THE HOMEBREW HANDBOOK

THE HOMEBREW HANDBOOK

75 RECIPES FOR THE
ASPIRING BACKYARD BREWER

DAVE LAW AND BESHLIE GRIMES

CICO BOOKS
LONDON NEW YORK

Published in 2012 by CICO Books
An imprint of Ryland Peters & Small Ltd
20–21 Jockey's Fields   519 Broadway, 5th Floor
London WC1R 4BW   New York, NY 10012

www.cicobooks.com

10 9 8 7 6 5 4 3 2 1

A CIP catalog record for this book is available from the Library of
Congress and the British Library.

ISBN: 978 1 908170 24 8

Printed in China

Editor: Caroline West
Designer: Ashley Western
Photographer: Gavin Kingcome
Stylist: Luis Peral-Aranda

For digital editions, visit www.cicobooks.com/apps.php

Measurements are given in metric and imperial
and are not interchangeable. Please follow one
set or the other.

Contents

INTRODUCTION
From Monk to Punk

If you have picked up this book, it is because you have a passion for beer big enough to make you want to brew it. I started brewing beer while at art school if only for two simple reasons—to have cheap beer to sell to mates and to get sloshed. Yes, it is an unfashionable thing to say these days but, let's be honest, we're all adults.

I like to think I have grown up since then (although my wife is probably the best judge of that). A beer for me now is more about taste, but it still helps me to relax and I still like the sensation of having one or two more than I should. There are dozens of great books on the subject of homebrewing, so what is it that makes this book different? Well, I'm going to try and cut through the mystique, the waffle, and the scientific attention to detail. Some books, for example, encourage wrapping duvets around wort buckets or hanging grain sacks along broomsticks. While the advice (and knowledge it is based on) is genuine, I hope to get you brewing with as simple and efficient an explanation and method as possible. After all, from the Sumerians through to the Victorians, beer production was little more than happy coincidence until Louis Pasteur (1822–1895) rocked up with his treatise on how to control those pesky yeasts. Until then everyone knew how to do it, but not why or how it really worked. The main events that need to occur are quite simple:

- The conversion of starches and carbohydrates to sugars
- The subsequent conversion of sugars to alcohol
- The addition of hops and adjuncts to add flavor and to preserve

Like many things, you can get as involved in the detail as you want, but it's not needed to begin with. Follow the simple steps, tips, and guidelines outlined in this book and you will be brewing your own in no time.

Today, you don't need to know all the complicated equations and go back to your school books to revisit algebra. You can pick up hop-rate apps and brewing programs on the Internet that will do all that for you. Your local brew-shop staff will usually be enthusiasts, too, and there are many fora to check out for help should you need it.

If I were to point out the single most likely factor that can wipe out your chances of brewing a decent beer—and jeopardizing your beery success—it would be dirt. Any muck in your equipment will undermine the chances of your homebrewed beer giving you a wide grin of satisfaction. So sanitize, sanitize, and sanitize again. And, please, don't just clean with your eyes—you will be amazed how many people do, much to their detriment.

Just For Fun: Words For Being Drunk

Trolleyed, bladdered, smashed, tanked up, hammered, tipsy, half cut, mashed, three sheets to the wind, puggled, scuttered, sloshed, wasted, plastered, maggoted, well oiled, spongy, ripped, pickled, wrecked, inebriated, merry, on a bender, had a skinfull, blotto, welly'd, stocius and totalled.

A Brief History of Beer

Beer brewing is probably the second oldest profession in the world. It started somewhere in Sumeria and Egypt in 6,000BC, from where it was carried to Europe by the Romans. It subsequently spread via the monks and their monasteries, abbeys, and mission stations across northern Europe.

In the past, people were literally "born into beer" because it was the safest source of clean water right up until the 19th century. Hops weren't introduced to the United Kingdom until around AD1400, although evidence shows that they were definitely in use in Germany and the Netherlands by AD800. Disciples of the hop, turn away now, because beer was made with adjuncts long before the hop took off. There are copious ancient recipes that include ingredients as diverse as heather, bog myrtle, cilantro (coriander), and tej (an Ethiopian mead or honey wine.) It has always been about experimenting and developing beer from the local ingredients available at the time.

If some brewers think of themselves today as a touch hardcore, spare a thought for King Wenceslas of Bohemia (1205–1253) who not only acted as God's representative on earth in order to repeal a law banning brewing in the 13th century, but also issued the death penalty to anyone caught exporting his beloved hops.

In 1516 William IV of Bavaria (1493–1550) became the world's first Environmental Health Officer when he introduced the very first food regulation—the Reinheitsdebot (more commonly known as the Bavarian/German Purity Law.) This ordered that beer could only be made from water, barley, and hops.

Sam Whitbread III (1830–1915) is credited with having pioneered the greatest improvement in brewing history when he brought Louis Pasteur to Britain in the 18th century. Pasteur's knowledge of yeast strains (and how to control them with temperature) led to beer being brewed all year round, with greater consistency and fewer accidents. Only a few years earlier, a dozen or so people had been killed in the East End of London when some brewing vats exploded.

The Industrial Revolution and the rise of the British Empire saw the British expand their beer production and export sales across the globe—the India Pale Ales (IPAs) being the best example. This now classic style was the catalyst that triggered the northern brewers of Germany and Holland to start moving away from their old, dark-beer roots and pioneer the styles that we now associate with bottom-fermented lagers. The British and their success with IPAs was soon eclipsed by brewers in the United States, who quickly rose to prominence and dominance, conquering all predecessors in market share if not necessarily in taste at this point.

Modern beer

By 1989 (while I was pretending to be the next Salvador Dalí), very few pubs in England sold anything other than the mainstream, multi-national brands of homogenous lager—sold on strength and refrigerated to such an extent as to remove the likelihood of tasting anything. Fast-forward 20 years and I am now a publican in London, with two award-winning, cask-ale-driven pubs. In the United Kingdom, lager has been in decline by some 25 per cent over the last five years with real ale being the only driver in the sector. Microbreweries have prospered since the Beer Orders of 1989, when Margaret Thatcher benevolently attempted to break up the power of the "Big Six" brewers.

Some good has come of this, however; namely, the increase in the number of microbrewers. Their numbers have risen sharply from around 252 in 1989 to about 848 today, with another four opening in London

Beer Facts from History

Medieval monks were convinced that the mortar for building churches was stronger mixed with ale rather than water.

Travelers in England are still entitled to claim ale and bread if they visit certain churches.

The Domesday Book (1086) records that the monks of St Paul's Cathedral in London brewed almost 70,000 UK gallons (84,000 US gallons) of ale that year.

Monks used the symbols X, XX, and XXX as symbols for the quality level of beer.

Through the Assize of Ale in 1266, ale-conners were appointed in UK boroughs and cities to test the quality of the ale and the accuracy of the measures being used.

By the early 14th century there was one "brewpub" for every 12 people in England.

Henry VIII gave the pint measurement its government stamp and inflicted the regulatory quagmire that is more commonly known in the United Kingdom today as Trading Standards.

Not so long ago—1810 to be precise—there were 48,000 alehouses for some eight million people in the UK. So, that's a pub for every 166 people. Where did it all go wrong?

John Wagner was the first to brew lager in North America. The year was 1840; the place was Philadelphia.

in the last year alone, thus bringing the number in the capital to 20. I know of at least another two in the pipeline—and nearly all of these microbrewers will have had humble beginnings as homebrewers.

The United States pre-empted this revolution, with microbrewers starting to emerge when canny operators spotted that the public were tired of what they were being offered by the giant corporates. Brewers such as Samuel Adams, Sierra Nevada, Geary's, Stones, and Dogfish Head have all exploded flavor options onto a market literally gagging for something new and different. One could be forgiven for suspecting that Dogfish Head and Stones may be the inspiration behind the self-acclaimed Punk-brewers, BrewDog in Scotland.

The Brewing Process

If there is anything that embodies the punk-band, "anyone-can-have-a-go" spirit of the 1980s, it is micro- or homebrewing. As I have said, it is in essence a relatively simple process to master.

When you design and make a beer it will be a reflection of you and how you were feeling at the time. Depending on that moment, it could be grossly scientific, obliging, innovative, and experimental, or profoundly personal. The deep-seated satisfaction of having created your own beer—a project undertaken from start to finish—is a constant joy. You can brew beer at home using a kit, malt extract, or the full-mash method.

From a kit

Beer-making kits have come a long way from the early insipid kits of the 1970s and 1980s with their extravagant claims. The choice is now massive, with regional and global brands widely available. They are worlds apart scientifically from their bell-bottomed cousins and impart confidence in people because they brew with consistent results and quality. This is the simplest method and all you have to do is what it says on the can.

From malt extract

The next step up, this method uses ready-prepared liquid malt extract as its base—simply add your choice of hops, adjuncts, and yeast. Additional malt grains can also be added, if you wish. This is probably the most popular method in the United States. It's commonly done on the stove (although your partner may not thank you for this) with a medium-sized pot, gives you a jump time-wise on the all-grain method, and is easier to cool down. Furthermore, can sizes in multiples of 1.5kg (3¼ lb) can assist in scaling down recipes if storage and/or time are an issue. It is, however, two to three times more expensive than using the all-grain method. (This method is covered well in practically every American book on homebrewing, as well as on the Internet.)

From the all-grain, full-mash, traditional method (The Daddy!)

For me, this is the way to go if you are serious about wanting to brew great-tasting beer that either replicates your favorites as much as possible or pushes the boundaries of beer boredom. It will cost you more in time and equipment, but with a bit of practice you will quickly be able to design and adapt beers to your own exacting requirements. The rewards will be deeply satisfying and hopefully soften the cost of the extra kit!

So, cut your teeth and master the traditional process. Don't be shy—the old adage that you learn from your mistakes is true. Be patient, and if you're worried about the brew not working out, scale down the ingredients. Do your apprenticeship for, say, five months and then it really is time to explore possibilities with other ingredients and techniques. You will progress from making good beer to great beer, I promise.

The three main concerns

When brewing beer at home, please bear the following points in mind because they can really have an impact on your chances of success.

CLEANLINESS Keep everything scrupulously clean if you want your beer to taste like something you'd drink rather than chuck on your fries (see page 17 for guidance on cleaning and sterilizing).

WATER A 4% ABV beer is roughly 96% water. How hard or soft your water supply is will have a massive impact on the taste of your chosen beer style. Either way, start with your faucet (tap) supply until you are more confident. If you are concerned about calcium and other chemical treatments, either filter or boil the water for 15–20 minutes. Gypsum salts (among other things) are often used by brewers to treat water. Treatment packs are available from your local homebrew store and you can play around endlessly with this aspect of homebrewing (see pages 30–31).

STORAGE How do you want to store your beer? In demijohns, poly-pins, mini-pins, barrels (firkins), kegs, or bottles? Unless exceptionally conditioned, beer in larger containers will tend to be less carbonated. Beer that is secondarily fermented in bottles will last longer, but will display different flavor notes and textures.

The six degrees

The mash, the sparge, the boil, fermentation, racking, and conditioning, and, oh yes, the best bit—the drinking. Oh, that's seven. No wonder I'm a publican! Seriously, though, you will need to master the following six key stages in order to produce beer that you will enjoy drinking.

1. THE MASH This is where you create your brewing wort by converting malt starch from grain into sugars. This is done by soaking the grain in heated water at about 68°C (154°F). I prefer to use an insulated mash tun with a hop strainer, but a basic bucket lined with a clean grain sack to create a giant tea bag will also do. The term "mash" is quite literal; you add the grain slowly to the pre-heated water (taken from your boiler) and stir, making sure that there is no dry grain. (Just like making creamy mashed potato, although your mash will look like porridge.)

Don't overdo it, though; too much stirring may result in cloudy beer because you will inevitably release too much starch, something the brewers of old didn't know. You want the grain hydrated but not saturated to the point of being waterlogged.

The temperature now needs to be maintained at 60–68°C (140–154°F). I prefer 66°C (151°F) for anything between 60–90 minutes. To adjust the temperature, just add hot or cold water accordingly. Like all good cooks, keep some pre-cooled and boiling water to hand.

2. THE SPARGE This is a Scottish invention, which, as you may imagine, was designed as the most efficient method of rinsing out as much of the converted sugars from the spent grain into the liquor to create the brewing wort. After draining off the majority of sweet malt liquor from the mash, we sparge by sprinkling water at a temperature of 75–80°C (167–175°F) over the surface of the mashed grain in order to extract as much malt sugar as possible and stop the sugar conversion. Please do not attempt any more stirring!

Pour the first and second draining back over the grain and top up with any spare liquor until the liquid is no longer sweet. The finger-licking test is adequate here (i.e. stick your finger under the faucet (tap) and lick it to see if the liquor is still sweet.) Once it isn't, turn off the tap. These run-offs are known as "runnings." Take your time here because you want lots of lovely fermentable sugars.

HOMEBREWING
Five Steps to Success

When brewing beer at home, you will be following these stages:

1. Malted barley is soaked in hot water (liquor) to extract the malt sugars that it contains.

2. This malt-sugar solution is boiled with hops.

3. The malt-hop infusion is cooled and yeast pitched to start fermentation.

4. The yeast ferments and eats the sugars, burping out carbon dioxide (CO_2) and ethyl alcohol.

5. Once the fermentation is complete, the beer can be bottled, kegged, or casked with a small amount of priming sugar to create some secondary fermentation and thus natural carbonation.

When doing this, be careful not to disturb the base grain bed because you do not want to draw off too much sediment. You can use a purpose-made sparger, a sanitized watering can, or a simple jug, just as long as you spread the liquor evenly over the grain surface. Let the liquor settle for around 10 minutes between each running, and don't pour in so much that it sits on the top of the grain. Don't squeeze your grain bag if you are using this method for mashing! Any spare liquor can be added to the boil as a top-up to that lost through evaporation.

3. THE BOIL Breweries conduct a boil in a copper, which, like a lot of brewing jargon, can be confusing, so beware. At home, the only difference between the all-grain and malt-extract methods is that for malt extract you can use a large pot on the stove instead of a cumbersome but dedicated gas or electric boiler.

Large, all-grain boilers for use with gas will help bring the brew up to temperature faster, and are more easily adjustable. Electric, kettle-like boiler elements have a habit of overheating and switching off. This is often due to hops clinging to the elements. Protect them with mesh or gauze or, better still, just stick with gas (although Burco boilers have concealed elements).

Don't forget to consider how you will cool the resultant boil down to 20°C (68°F). I recently upgraded to a 55-litre (12-gallon/14½-US-gallon) boiler, which was, of course, too big for a bath of ice. Homebrewers used to allow the boil to cool over night. Alternatively, you can rig up a cooling element, which is readily available from homebrew stores.

4. PRIMARY FERMENTATION This is the process of adding or pitching your yeast to convert the sugars in the brewing wort into alcohol and carbon dioxide. There are a wide variety of brewer's yeasts available and they come either dry or wet. You can, of course, cultivate yeast from beer bottles or from the cask beer at your local pub, which is especially useful if you are trying to clone/replicate your favorite beer (see page 33). Yeast cultivation is also explained in more depth on these pages. For sheer convenience and speed, I prefer the reliability of "smack-pack" yeasts, which are readily available online or from your local brew store.

5. RACKING This is brewer-speak for transferring the beer after primary fermentation is completed into your desired choice of container. Whether you decide to use

Mixing the water and malt

The brewing wort

Preparing for sparging

bottles, barrels, pins, mini-pins, or demijohns in order to "rack" your beer, it is crucial to consider where you will conduct this part of the gig. It must be sterile or you risk spoiling the beer. You need the fermenter to be above the receptacle of choice by a good 30cm (12in) to ensure gravity helps the flow rate. It's a good idea to move the container into place a couple of hours before siphoning in order to let any sediment drop to the bottom. It will improve your chances of "bright"beer (of course, if sediment is your thing, don't bother), as will skimming off any yeast from the surface.

Get a siphon with a faucet (tap) on the end so that you can control the flow-rate going into the container. One with a U-tube configuration at one end will help stop any sediment getting sucked along. Traditionally, you would have to place the U-tube in the bin, open the tap, and suck on it to the get beer through. This is fine if it's just you drinking the beer, but I recommend using a fermenter container with a tap at the bottom if you plan to move on commercially, or share with friends. Remember that there can be a great many germs in your mouth, so you need to keep everything as clean as possible. Lactobacilli are the most common beer-wreckers, with wild yeasts close behind, so try to keep spills to a minimum because this is the ideal opportunity for it to spread. Run your siphon into a pitcher (jug) first to minimize any spillages.

6. CONDITIONING Conditioning is the secondary fermentation that occurs in your chosen container, producing the carbon dioxide gas that gives beer its sparkle or slight fizz. For the purposes of secondary fermentation, I believe cask ale is king. It has a more rounded, fuller flavor that just can't be replicated by draught, bottling, or even bottle conditioning due to the "live" secondary fermentation and liberal dry hopping. The diversity and complexity of flavors paired with the uniqueness of cask is a great selling point for beers produced in the United Kingdom.

A vital part of the craft, a publican will mature a cask in the cellar. Although you can also do this, you'll have to drink it within three to five days once beer has been drawn off (36-pint pins are ideal). Depending on how "au naturel" you want your beer—and if you can contain your excitement—you can just container the beer and leave it for another couple of weeks to "condition" for the same effect. Any residual sugars will be enough to start a secondary ferment as long as the container is properly sealed.

So, only add as much priming sugar as is absolutely necessary, as per the manufacturer's instructions. The sugar feeds on the remaining yeast, creating carbon dioxide. Put in too much and you get exceptionally frothy beer or—in the case of bottles—exploding glass.

If you use sugar, add roughly half a teaspoon to every 500ml (18 fl oz) of beer. Leave approximately 2.5cm (1in) of space at the top of the bottle when you are filling it and then cap as per the manufacturer's instructions. When you are satisfied that your containers are all tightly capped or barrel-sealed, keep in a warm place for a week at 20°C (68°F). Wipe down with sanitizer to get rid of any splashed beer. Then move them on to a cellar or adapted fridge for a couple of days at 12–15°C (54–60°F). Any yeast produced by the secondary fermentation will help "drop" the beer "bright" if the beer is kept cool. If you aren't worried about clarity, then go with it.

7. LUCKY SEVEN—DRINKING! Sample your beer after a week or so. If it is too "flat," move it back to a warm place and try again in a few days. If it is too lively, try chilling it before you pour it. If the beer is below 10°C (50°F), it is likely to suffer "chill haze;" if above 15°C (60°F), it is less likely to settle and drop "bright."

More yeast will be created during the secondary fermentation, so, in the case of bottles, try not to disturb it when pouring the beer into your glass. If the beer gushes, it is either highly conditioned or too warm. If it's the former, then happy days—just give it a couple more days to settle. If it's the latter, cool it down fast! Top-pressure and cask-breathers may assist, but keep this quiet from your beer-head mates.

Pouring and tasting your beer

I'm not going to insult your intelligence. If you don't know how to pour beer by now, ask your mother. If, on tasting, you find your beer hasn't turned out as you wanted, don't be disheartened. There are so many variables when brewing beer. At this level no two batches will be the same and things inevitably go wrong. Regional brewers and microbrewers often have to pour beer down the drain in pursuit of perfection. Start small until you have gained confidence.

A note on lagering

The process for brewing lager is exactly the same as for ale, except that lager is fermented at a much lower temperature (0–5°C/32–41°F) and ideally needs different yeasts. The primary fermentation takes twice as long and the finished article then needs to be stored for weeks, sometimes months, to properly "lager" (which is German for "store.") This is why it is beyond most homebrewers. Give it a go, though; I am sure that you will be able to brew something fairly flavorsome.

Essential Equipment

Obtaining the right equipment for homebrewing is a worthwhile investment and will give the best results. Here, I have provided a list of the most useful items that will bring success and pleasure to your homebrewing experiments.

AERATION KIT Consisting of a pump, filter, diffusion stone, and tubing, this important piece of kit introduces the oxygen to the wort that is necessary for the yeast to start the fermentation process.

AIRLOCKS These are simple to use and make it easy to check whether your beer is producing CO_2. Look at the water line to see if the gas is bubbling through.

ALUMINUM (aluminium) stock pots These can be used instead of the mash tun for mashing, although this method is a little more tricky and, for the sake of a small investment, I would not want to recommend that someone try to strain the boiling mash, especially considering that you may well be lifting huge pots of boiling hot malt and water.

BOILER A large vessel (heated using gas or electricity) that holds a large volume of liquid, keeping it at the boil for the required time.

BOTTLES Any shape of bottle is fine, but make sure that you don't use a screw or twist-off cap.

Bottles also need to be brown. (If you can get hold of swing-top bottles, then you will not need to get a bottle capper.)

BOTTLE CAPPER A bench-crown capper is the easiest to use because it is fixed to your worktop surface, although two-handed cappers are more common. Both types of bottle capper can be found on homebrewing supply websites or in your local homebrew store.

BOTTLE DRYER Holding 45–80 bottles, a bottle dryer or tree enables you to keep drying bottles clean.

BOTTLE FILLER A great gadget, although not essential, a bottle filler takes the place of a hose clamp for bottling your beer. Attach to one end of the siphon tubing. When the end of the wand hits the bottom of the bottle, a valve opens and lets the beer flow through.

BRUSHES A must-have for

Aeration kit

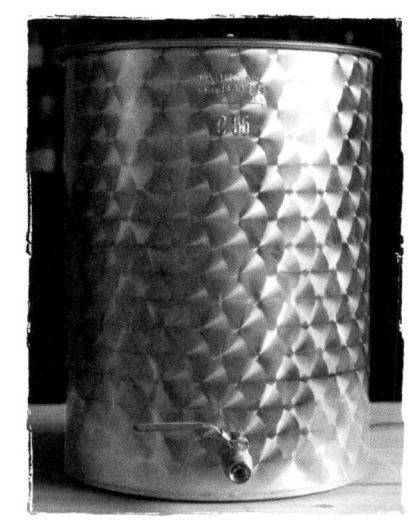

Boiler

14

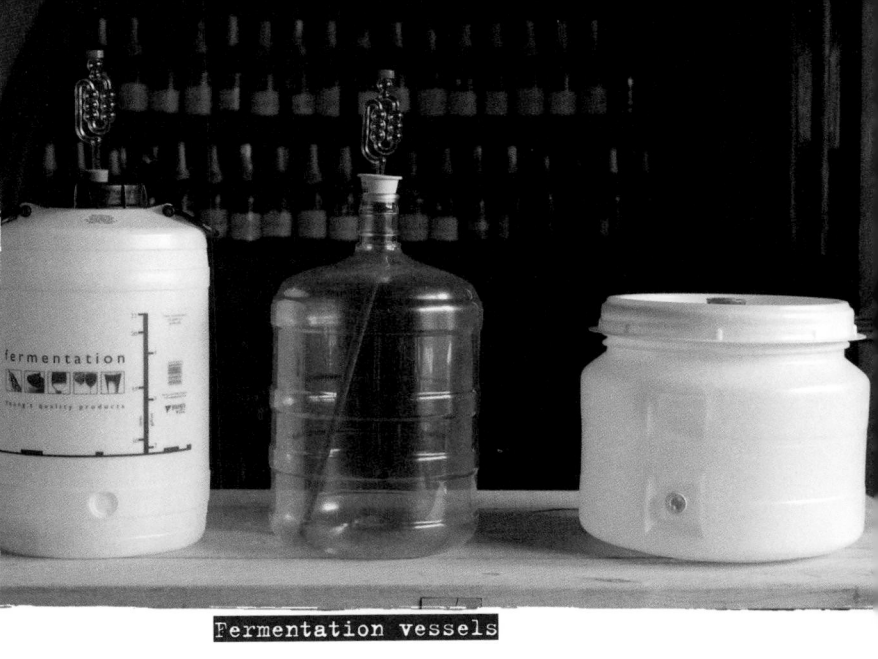

Bottle capper

Fermentation vessels

thoroughly cleaning tubing, airlocks, and fermenter necks. Ideally, you will need a carboy brush, pipe cleaners, and a narrow nylon brush. All available from homebrew stores.

BUCKET For sterilizing all of your equipment. It needs to be big enough to hold a couple of gallons of sanitizer and your equipment.

FERMENTATION VESSELS Glass or plastic carboys or demijohns can be used for primary or secondary fermentation. If using for primary fermentation, use an airlock/blow-off valve as well. Also refers to large, food-grade, plastic fermentation vessels with an airtight lid suitable for attaching a bung and airlock/blow-off valve. Ideal for secondary fermentation.

FERMENTING BUCKETS Use food-grade buckets (capacity 25 litres/5½ gallons/6½ US gallons) with tight-fitting lids for primary fermentation. Try to get buckets with a tap fitted for ease of use. They should be easily obtainable from all good homebrew stores.

GRAIN BAG A large, very fine mesh

bag required for holding all of the grain during the mash. Always use a nylon bag as these are usually finer meshed and will last a lot longer than the muslin variety. The finer the mash, the fewer particles are left in the wort. The grain bag will need to measure at least 50 x 50cm (20 x 20in).

HOSE CLAMP A device that is useful for opening and closing tubing while bottling. Always make sure that the clamp can click completely shut and fits the tubing.

HYDROMETER AND TUBE If possible, try to get a hydrometer that can also measure temperature, especially as a hydrometer reading is only accurate at 15°C (60°F). You should also be able to acquire a trial tube with a base that can be helpful when measuring specific gravity. This is an inexpensive but essential piece of a homebrewer's kit.

KEGS I like the bottom-tap keg that holds nearly 26 litres (5½ gallons/ 6½ US gallons) and has a 10cm (4in) neck opening, which allows for easy cleaning. The screw cap carries a pressure release and a

CO_2 introduction valve to enable excess gas from over-priming to be released automatically. Additional gas can also be introduced to keep up internal pressure. A great keg especially if your brew needs a while to mature and clear.

MASH PADDLE A device essential for mixing in the strike water and breaking up dough balls (dry pockets of malt) during the mashing process. A mash paddle is a basic piece of brewing equipment, and it is difficult to do all-grain brewing without one. Most real homebrew enthusiasts will craft their own brew paddle from oak or maple, but never use pine as this will impair the flavor of the beer. It will need to be fairly long and the base oblong in shape with six to eight large holes drilled into it. If you are making your own paddle, fill the pot a gallon at a time and mark the volumes on the paddle in gallon increments. You'll then be able to see roughly how much wort you have at any one time.

MASH TUN These are now easy to

Mash tun

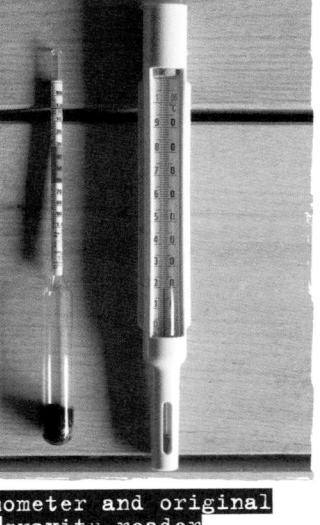

Thermometer and original gravity reader

Tubing for bottling

get hold of through the Internet or a homebrew store. They take a lot of the pain out of boiling up malt on your stove and the inevitable sticky boil-overs that happen. Mash tuns are highly efficient and capable of mashing up to 10kg (22lb) of grain. They usually come complete with tap and integral wort separator and with a capacity of 30 litres (6½ gallons/8 US gallons).

RACKING CANE An essential bit of kit for siphoning beer into bottles, usually long enough to fit 23-litre (5-gallon/6-US-gallon) fermenters. I opt for the plastic variety, but metal ones are also available. Also, any residue is easier to detect in the clear plastic types. There are some with a built-in suction chamber that can start a siphon without you having to suck on the tube and, as we have pointed out elsewhere, earlier sanitation is key, so it is not a great idea to introduce bacteria at this point.

SCALES (digital) I cannot stress

enough the importance of buying a set of scales that will measure kilograms and grams. Once you have bought your full list of grain, hops and adjuncts, you will not want to waste a single gram, so do yourself a favor and invest in a set of digital scales!

STRAINER Just a normal fine-meshed sieve will work well, since this is needed to strain out the trub. I often use a metal sieve.

TEMPERATURE CONTROLLER If you would like to go all out, pick up an old refrigerator and keep it solely for your lager development; all you need to do is plug the fridge into the controller and plug the controller into the wall. Fix the built-in thermometer in the fridge and set the controller to a lagering temperature of 13°C (55°F) for primary and 4°C (40°F) for secondary fermentation (usually one month). The controller will do its thing, and turn off and on as needed to achieve and maintain the correct temperature.

THERMOMETER If you can't get

hold of a combined hydrometer/ thermometer, then a metal thermometer will do. Don't be tempted to buy a glass one as they break fairly easily.

TUBING You will need food-grade vinyl tubing, which can be seen through. The tubing should ideally be thrown away after 10 brews and new ones bought. You will need a wide tube to use as a blow-off hose and a narrow one which will be connected to your racking cane. Any good homebrew store will be able to advise you on this. (Wide tubing should be approximately 2.5cm/1in inside diameter and narrow tubing 1cm/⅜in inside diameter.)

TURKEY BASTER Great for obtaining small samples to taste or to use as samples to find your specific gravity.

CLEANING KIT

To make great beer, clean and sanitize obsessively. Make sure you have a sterilizing bucket, some sterilizing chemicals (for making up a sanitizing solution,) a dish-cloth, and a spritzer bottle.

Sterilization

If you are serious about making really great beer, then read on. What you learn here will make all the difference between having drinkable beer and pouring it directly down the drain. Sanitize, sanitize, and then sanitize again; boring this may be, but you will thank me later!

Make up a solution of sanitizer in a bucket and submerge all of your brewing equipment. Sanitizing solution can be obtained from your homebrew store, whether you opt for a liquid or a powder. I personally prefer a chlorine-based powder. Just follow the manufacturer's instructions. Then, put some sanitizing solution into a spritzer so that you can clean worktops and do any last-minute sanitation jobs. Keep a dish-cloth solely for beer-making and don't use your usual kitchen one because this will contain incalculable numbers of beer-destroying bacteria.

Anything that is alive and thriving before the boil will be dead afterward, so don't become obsessive before the main event. At this stage, all of the equipment just needs to be clean—after the boil is when problems can occur. After the boil everything that comes into contact with the beer needs to be sterilized; that is, everything including the fermenting buckets, tubing, and valves need to have been soaked in the sterilizing solution. If you follow the advice above, then the outcome is potentially going to be a good one. Good luck!

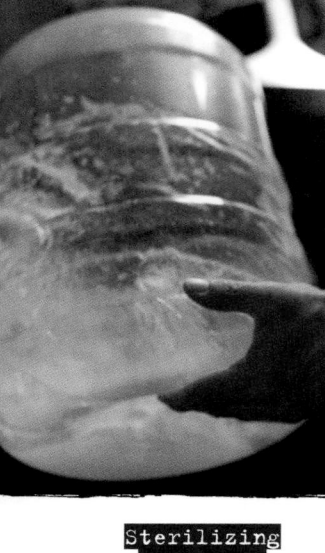

Sterilizing equipment before use

Sterilizing with boiling water

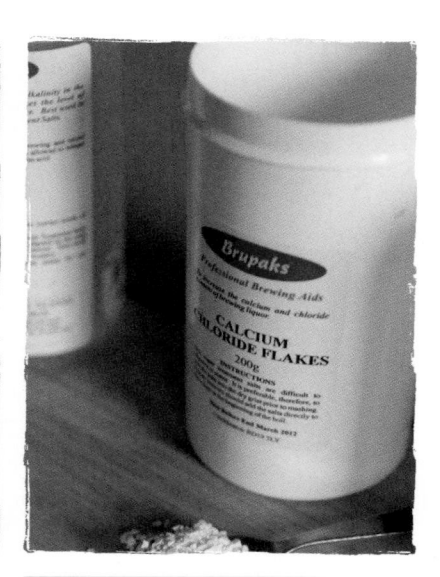

Sterilizing chemicals

Essential Ingredients

In my book, the saying "you are what you eat" is bang on. So, using the best ingredients when brewing beer is vital to success—always try to eliminate as many areas as possible where you might slip up. Wherever I can, I opt for organic ingredients.

Water

This can be a hugely complex subject. While there is no doubt that good brewing liquor improves the extraction of malt sugars, enhances hop utilization, and gives a better chance of a cleaner ferment, it must be remembered that for hundreds of years brewers made perfectly good beers with no water treatment other than boiling.

Much is made of the generally accepted belief that Burton water is the best brewing water in the world. This myth has been exposed by the great beer writer of our times, Roger Protz, who recently unearthed public supply charts dating back to the height of IPA fame that appear to dispel the claims for Burton. The charts show great variation in carbonates, suggesting that the so-called naturally occurring gypsous water was not as idyllic as the marketing would suggest. Today's public supply charts show an alarming disparity between day and night. At night there is a high nitrate and sodium ion concentration. Taking this into account, you may want to consider using your mains water supply during the day when nitrate levels are lower, as these will batter your yeast and affect your results.

Water is all too often overlooked by home brewers, but the liquor's impact on your brew cannot be denied. This is mainly due to the levels of calcium carbonate, sodium, and nitrates that may be present. With brew science having come on so much in the last 10 years, technology and the improved quality of ingredients really do give us the ability to produce beer on a level playing field with our commercial cousins. So, it would be a shame not to nail the last piece of the jigsaw into place by failing to consider the water used for your brewing liquor.

Before letting this descend into a chemistry lesson, I would suggest fitting a good filter to your mains supply, such as the FilterStream by SodaStream. This removes chlorine, polyphenols, and heavy metals, etc. No plumbing is required, either; just replace the cartridges as per the manufacturer's instructions. Filtration is the easiest method by far and will also catch other nasties, such as rust and sand.

Alternatively, boil your water supply for 15–20 minutes to force out the suspended chemicals. You are aiming for a pH of around 5.3–5.6 for bottom-fermenting beers and 5.0–5.1 for top-fermenting ones. So, if you don't boil or filter, you will shove this up to something much higher. Don't forget to clean out your boiler afterward to remove the chemical scum and sediment (we don't want this reintroducing itself.)

If you fancy playing around with water quality, then turn to pages 30–31 for the full-on, teacher bit on this fascinating subject.

Malt

The most popular grain used for beer production is barley, although wheat grain is also used, particularly in Belgian, Weiss, and Wit beers. Today, barley must exhibit a range of specialized properties in order to meet a brewer's exacting standards. It is analyzed by variety and for nitrogen and moisture content before malting is even attempted. Barley is the most commonly malted grain due to the diastatic or "enzymatic power" of the grain. This generally refers only to malts—grains that have begun to germinate. The act of germination results in the production of a number of enzymes, such as amylase, which convert

starch into sugar; thereby, sugars can be extracted from the barley's starches simply by soaking the grain in water at a controlled temperature. This is called mashing.

The grain's husk is incredibly hard, so malters have to add water, heat, and aeration to make the grain germinate. Once germinated, the growth is stopped there by a process called dry kilning, making it easier to develop the enzymes that convert the starches to sugars. This is also vital for the production of enzymes that break down protein for conversion to alcohol by yeast.

In general, the hotter a grain is kilned, the less its diastatic activity. Consequently, only lightly colored grains can be used as base malts (main malt), with Munich malt being the darkest base malt generally available. Once the malting of the grain has taken place, it can be roasted to produce varying levels of sweetness and color.

Malt grains have to be crushed for brewing purposes, but you can buy them uncrushed if you want to add more time to your craft. The most common base malt is pale malt or, in the case of lager, pale lager malt, which is sweet. In contrast, the crystal malt used in the production of British bitters will have been slightly roasted to produce a sweet, toffee-like flavor and a browner color.

The majority of brewers, commercial or otherwise, use pale malt as the main constituent of their grist. The grist or "grain bill" (which is also sometimes referred to as the mash roll) is the sum of malts, grains, and adjuncts that are put through the mash. The combination of these constituents will determine the color, malt flavor, and alcoholic strength of the beer.

Another general rule of thumb is that around 90 per cent of a grist will be pale malt—hence the term "base malt"—with only 10 per cent of specialty malts and adjuncts being added to vary the degree of color or flavor.

The color scale for malts is evaluated by the Standard Reference Method (SRM), Lovibond (°L), American Society of Brewing Chemists (ASBC), or European Brewery Convention (EBC) standards. While SRM and ASBC originate in North America and EBC in Europe, all three systems can be found in use throughout the world. (See page 20 for an example of a color-scale chart.)

Coloring malts are similar to base malts but have been kilned for longer. This gives them a darker color and a more distinct character. Examples of coloring malts include amber malt (60–100 EBC), brown malt (130–150 EBC), chocolate malt (500–1350 EBC), and black malt (1400–1600 EBC).

Malt

SRM/LOVIBOND	EXAMPLE	BEER COLOR	EBC
2	Pale lager		4
3	German Pilsener		6
4	Pilsner Urquell		8
6			12
8	Weissbier		16
10	Bass pale ale		20
13			26
17	Dark lager		33
20			39
24			47
29	Porter		57
35	Stout		69
40			79
70	Imperial stout		138

Malt range

Nothing but the best barley is used for malting. Once malted, the barley should still be sweet in taste and smell, as well as able to float in water. Malt is roasted light or dark, although you will find it sold with various descriptions and names as is shown in the malt chart on the opposite page. Do not be afraid to ask for advice at your local homebrew store if you are in any doubt about the best malt to use for a particular beer. However, bear in mind that the strength of the beer is imparted by pale malt (i.e. the base malt) because this gives the highest yield. Crystal and/or caramel malts will add depth and substance to sweeter beers, amber and brown malts will have a similar effect but, being slightly darker, will give a smoother finish and deeper color. Black malt is heavily roasted, delivering a very rich flavor that is particularly good for stouts and porters. Finally, roast barley, although not as rich as black malt, is needed to produce a dry finish to certain beers and dry stouts.

PALE MALT is dried at temperatures designed to preserve all the brewing enzymes in the grain. This keeps down the cost of kilning, making it the least expensive and most popular malt available (with the exception of lager malt).

MILD MALT is mainly derived from Triumph barley and is commonly used in Europe for lager malt, as well as for milds in the United Kingdom. It is kilned slightly hotter than pale malt for a fuller, sweeter flavor.

ACID MALT contains lactic acid, which will lower the pH of your mash, creating the same effect as adding gypsum to the liquor, but it is softer on the palate. It is normally used for making top-end lagers.

PILSNER MALT is kilned slowly at low temperatures until dry and then toasted at 80°C (175°F). It is very pale, with a strong sweet flavor and high enzyme content, making it a good base malt. It is often added to pale beers for flavor and high yields.

VIENNA MALT is kilned at higher temperatures to Pilsner and is therefore darker and more aromatic. Also used as a base malt, it will add both color and flavor to Vienna and Marzen beer styles.

MUNICH MALT is both darker and fuller flavored than Vienna. It has a high enzyme content despite its high-temperature kiln and is an essential ingredient for German bock beers.

MELANOIDIN MALT from Bamberg, in Germany, has an aromatic, full flavor and is slightly lighter in color than crystal malt. It is used to make medium dark beers, particularly Munich lagers.

CRYSTAL MALT is a British variety. It can be pale or dark, but averages 150–160 EBC, provides a strong, nutty, caramel taste and adds depth to the flavor of the beer.

HONEY MALT is much like crystal malt, but softer on the palate due to its slightly lighter roasted overtone.

MALT CHART WORKING ACROSS THE CHART ARE THE VARIOUS NAMES FOR THE SAME MALT OR ADJUNCT.

2-row pale	Pilsen	Lager			
Pale ale	Maris otter	Pearl			
Stout malt	Halcyon				
Ashburne	Mild ale	Vienna	Aromatic		
Bonlander	Munich	Munich I			
Vienna					
Munich 10	Munich	Munich II	Dark Munich		
Dextrine	Carafoam				
Victory	Amber	Melanoidin	Biscuit	Kiln Amber	
Crystal 10	Caramalt	Carapils	Caramalt	Carahell	Light caramel
Crystal 20	Carared	Caravienne	Caramel Vienna		
Crystal 30	Pale crystal	Caramunich I	Carastan	Caramel amber	
Crystal 40	Crystal malt 40–50	Caramunich II	Carastan	Medium caramel	Caramel Munich 40
Crystal 60	Crystal malt 60–70	Caramunich III	Caramunich	Dark caramel	Caramel Munich 60
Crystal 80	Dark crystal malt 85–95	Crystal malt	Dark caramunich		
Crystal 90	Dark crystal				
Crystal 120	Dark crystal	Dark crystal II (118–124)	Cararoama	Special B	Caramel Munich 120
Special roast	Brown malt	Kiln Amber			
Extra special	Kiln coffee				
Pale chocolate	Carafa I				
Chocolate	Carafa II				
Black patent	Carafa III	Black malt	Roasted malt	Kiln black	
Roasted barley	Black barley				
Roasted wheat	Chocolate wheat				
Wheat					
Dark wheat					
Crystal wheat	Carawheat	Caramel wheat			
Roasted rye					
Rye malt					
Caramel rye malt					
Oat malt					
Peated malt	Smoked malt				

STOUT MALT is actually quite pale in spite of its name. A stout's color comes from roasted malt and usually roasted, unmalted barley.

AMBER MALT is a toasted form of pale malt, which is used with other malts due to its low enzyme content. You should use this for English brown ales, milds, and old ales.

SMOKED MALT originates from Germany and is popular in the production of Alt/Rauchbiers. It is usually smoked with beech, but there is a Scottish version that is smoked over peat. It is a powerful malt, so should be used sparingly.

BROWN MALT is not too dissimilar to smoked malt, and is used in dark ales.

COFFEE MALT will impart a distinctive coffee aroma, as its name suggests, so be very careful when choosing the quantity to use.

BLACK MALT is kilned to a very high temperature, leaving it with no enzymes and less starch, and thus little fermentable extract. Very bitter, it is used for both flavor and color in dark beers.

CHOCOLATE MALT is similar to black malt but softer. It has a smoky rather than bitter flavor, has no enzymatic content and is used with roasted, unmalted barley in dark beers.

Adjuncts

These are those grains used in the grist that are not derived from malted barley. Unmalted grains are sometimes used, but these require mashing for over 90 minutes to extract the necessary sugars.

ROAST BARLEY gives stout its burnt, bitter essence and ruby-black hue. It weighs in at 1600–1700 EBC, so, as you can imagine, it should be used sparingly or it will be an overpowering flavor in your beer.

BLACK BARLEY is roasted to a greater degree than roast barley, which produces a pronounced and very strong burnt flavor and darker color.

FLAKED BARLEY offers a grainy flavor and helps with head retention. It can be used in large quantities for bitters and dark beers, but can cause haze problems in paler styles.

TORRIFIED BARLEY is made from heating barley kernels. With a distinctive flavor, it is also good for head retention.

Wheat malt

When flaked, wheat provides the protein haze characteristically common in Wheat/Weiss beers and is also used in British styles for head retention in which it can make up 50 per cent of a grain bill. Torrified wheat is used for a tighter, creamy head retention.

FLAKED OR TORRIFIED MAIZE is commonly used by the British to lighten the color without changing the taste too much; think Stella Artois.

RYE will provide the very distinctive, spicy dryness associated with beer like the German Roggenbier. Like wheat, rye has no husk, and is difficult to malt, so doesn't form a filter bed in the mash.

SORGHUM AND MILLET are gluten-free grains popular in African and Indian brewing, often creating dark, hazy beers suitable for those allergic to gluten. I don't have any recipes for beer associated with these grains, such as Chhaang, Pomba, or Namibian Oshikundu, so if you find any please forward them on!

RICE AND CORN are often used as substitutes for malt grain by commercial brewers. They are pretty flavorless, but a much cheaper way to replace malt or sugar in order to increase strength in a beer, but not the body. This "thinning out" was jumped on by the giants of the North American brewing industry to create a lager style now diametrically opposed to those of Germany or the Czech Republic.

BUCKWHEAT AND QUINOA are not grains but do contain high enough levels of protein and starch without gluten to enable the production of beer suitable for those suffering from coeliac disease.

WEYERMANN MALT OF BAMBERG offer a range of fantastic specialty malts as well as a range of organics.

Sugar

This should ideally come under the adjunct section, but, like all aspects of brewing, it can create a lengthy thesis. As we are trying not to go there, we will limit it to a few paragraphs.

Unlike the complex starches in malt, which need to be broken down into simpler forms through malting and mashing, sugars such as demerara are practically there already. They can be added to both the boil and the fermentation. How much you use will

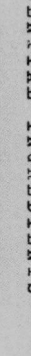

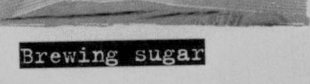

Brewing sugar

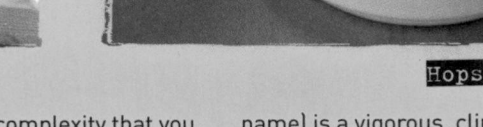

Hops

depend on the alcohol content and complexity that you require. Add too much, and you can end up with cider- or champagne-style dryness or a poorly balanced beer, so be careful.

Essentially—excluding extreme circumstances—you shouldn't be aiming to add more than 20 per cent in adjunct sugar above and beyond the malt sugar you have extracted from the grain. If you want a strong beer above 10% ABV, then add the sugar to the fermentation. Also, be careful to check your yeast spec to make sure that it won't be overcome by the adjunct and not ferment the beer properly. The later you add the sugars, the more aroma and flavor will be instilled in your beer. When adding sugars to the fermentation, sterilize them in hot water until they dissolve and allow to cool to 27°C (81°F) before adding to the fermenting beer. Roughly 500g (18oz) of sugar will add ten points or so to the original gravity.

You can use the following sugars: pure cane sugar, demerara sugar, Belgian amber candi sugar, dark brown sugar, Belgian light candi sugar, and light brown sugar.

Hops

Hops counterbalance the sweetness of malt. There are three main types: bittering hops (added at the start of the boil), aroma hops (added at the end of the boil,) and, of course, dual-purpose hops. Additionally, hops act as a great natural preservative. In fact, the combination of high hop rates together with high alcohol content created the antibiotic effect that allowed the first IPAs to survive the long journeys from Britain to India. In the United Kingdom there are approximately 18 indigenous varieties of hops.

The hop or *Humulus lupulus* (to use the botanical name) is a vigorous, climbing herbaceous perennial that will grow up to 5.4m (18ft) high if you let it. The female cones are more commonly used. It is a highly resinous plant related to hemp. The resins are made up of two main acids: alpha and beta. The alpha acid gives flavor and the beta acid provides aroma. Beta acids should nearly always be introduced toward the end of the boil as over-oxidization can result in off-flavors akin to rotten vegetables or cooked corn. Dual-purpose hops have enough alpha acid for bitterness, but also enough essential oils to offer flavor and aroma. For increased flavor, add more hops toward the end of the boil.

Noble hops are practically that of appellation/designation, being Hallertau, Saaz, Spalt, and Tettnang. Lager traditionally contains these hops. English ales, on the other hand, use Fuggle, Golding, Target, Pioneer, or Progress. New World varieties popular with craft brewers today include Cascade, Citra, Chinook, Columbia, Mount Hood, Nelson Sauvin, and Willamette.

The supply of hops can be erratic, as the alpha acids and harvest vary naturally from year to year. If you can't get a certain type or the same AA (apparent attenuation) percentage, don't fret; simply substitute it with either a higher volume or a different variety. Happy Hops, Get Hoppy, and Brew Target are good app software that will remove the pain of working this out, but it's quite simple, so here's the equation for the calculation anyway:

New substitute hop weight =
recipe weight x AA% of recipe
divided by the new substitute hop AA

23

Higher-quality worts tend to utilize less bitterness, so you may need to up the quantity of hops. A rough guide is 10 per cent more boil hops for every ten points of original gravity over 1.060.

As you will see from the sample recipes, there are endless ways to promote more hops, even after the wort has boiled. This generally takes the form of "dry hopping" using pellets or whole-leaf hops as fermentation dies down or during the storage transfer. Hop-oil derivatives can also be added at about 50mg (0.001oz) per 23 litres/5 gallons/6 US gallons) to significantly increase the hop profile, although the latter is frowned upon by many a brewer.

Traditionally, brewers would use a bittering hop, possibly two, and one aroma hop. Today, as you will see, some brewers are using six hops or more for bittering, with more hops added halfway through for flavor, and numerous mixes of beta and dual-purpose hops at the end of the boil. There are no limits to the changes to what was once an accepted principle.

Once you build up a collection of hops, it may be advantageous to store them in a freezer. Don't buy hops in a transparent bag, but foil-wrapped instead to ensure freshness. UV light plays havoc with the hop oils, which is why brown bottles are used for storing beer. (For a full briefing chart on hops with descriptions, origins, and type, as well as suggested substitutes see pages 30–31.)

Yeast

Yeast

Yeasts are largely forgotten about compared with the other main constituents of beer, perhaps because many don't think the choice of yeasts will change the flavor profile considerably. However, this is not true (although I have been somewhat guilty of this myself.) I recently attended an event held by Charles Faram and Wye Hops Ltd. (and sponsored by the National Hop Association of Britain,) where the same ale recipe was brewed using four different yeasts by Fermentis (yeast suppliers to the trade.) The resulting impact on flavor variation was shocking, particularly the one using T-58: it offered very strong, spicy, fruity, and woody notes to an ale—from a yeast usually associated with stouts and barley wine.

As a brewer you can still influence your beer at fermentation stage, depending on the yeast you select, the way you rehydrate it, how you pitch it, and at what temperature you do so (not forgetting whether you are using a fresh starter or a re-pitch.) When choosing a yeast, always consider the alcohol content. High levels of alcohol are toxic to yeast and can kill it, stopping

further fermentation. Strong beers need a yeast with good apparent attenuation (AA), which is the posh word for the measurable amount of sugars that a yeast can eat. An average yeast will attenuate 65 to 75 per cent of the sugar suspended in the liquid. One solution is to pitch more or another type of yeast as fermentation is beginning to slow down, which helps to ferment higher-than-average sugar levels. An example would be to begin with an ale yeast for the first half of fermentation and then pitch a wine or Champagne yeast when you are halfway to your intended final gravity. In this way, the beer will retain more of the ale characteristics than the dryness associated with wine and cider.

Whichever yeast you choose, make sure you prepare it in advance because cooled wort is at high risk of infection and you don't want it standing around waiting to get spoilt. (For a more comprehensive guide to the different yeast types and how to use them, as well as advice on how to culture your own, see page 30.)

If you would like to clone or replicate a favorite beer (see page 33), you can culture the individual brewer's strain via a bottle of that beer or indeed a "green" and "undropped" barrel at your local pub. Dry yeasts used to receive a bad press because they picked up wild yeasts while going through the drying process, but technological improvements mean that this should no longer be a problem.

Personally, I love the WY Yeasts, especially the "smack-packs." They are more expensive but so convenient, and provide a great selection of specialty strains. Don't forget that your local commercial brewers may be willing to sell you their strain for a much lower rate. This goes for a lot of other ingredients, too!

Fruits, herbs, and other things-spike it as you like it!

So, you've mastered the traditional principles, you are making consistent beer, are comfortable with the permutations, familiar with the varying styles, and know your palate. Now it's time to ignore convention and start being imaginative in your choice of additional ingredients. The possibilities are endless, from subtle changes with a Bock using lemongrass and galangal to Heffeweiss with blood orange or juniper.

Perceived wisdom has constraints, which will hold you back. Yes, Black IPA is not strictly an India Pale Ale, but by adding darker malts into the grist, some of the brewing guys (such as those at the Windsor & Eton Brewery, in England) are challenging tradition and creating a talking point. It may not be to a purist's taste but anything that promotes more talk about beer, pubs and the community is all good by me. Ask yourself, would the same critics of Black IPA have bemoaned the aggressive hopping rates of the original IPAs or do they cry about US Double IPAs?

You don't have to be quirky to change a dynamic within a recipe. At the same time, testing yourself will not only improve your knowledge of how and why certain ingredients affect the final outcome, but it may also lead to some damn-fine nirvana. Remember using fruits, flowers, and herbs is not a new thing. Historically, beers were flavored with virtually anything to hand long before the use of hops. Williams Bros of Alloa, in Scotland, have been going since 1993. Having researched some indigenous historic recipes, they created some esoteric gems, such as Heather Fraoch and Kelpie Seaweed Ale. Similarly, young and emerging brewers continue to experiment. Ones to watch in the United Kingdom, for example, are Brodies, Dark Star, Downton, Kernel, Saltaire, and Thornbridge.

Some herbs, flowers, and spices used in brewing

Bitter orange
Blackberries
Blood orange
Cardamom
Chamomile
Cherries
Chilies
Chocolate nibs
Cilantro (coriander)
Cinnamon
Citrus fruit peel
Cloves
Cocoa
Elderflowers
Fennel seed
Figs
Ginger
Ground coffee
Heather
Hibiscus flowers
Juniper
Lavender
Lemon verbena
Lemongrass
Nutmeg
Passion fruits
Peaches
Raspberries
Rose hips
Saffron
Sarsaparilla
Strawberries

WOODCHIPS The effect that woodchips have on flavor has been well known throughout the brewing industry for many years. Using woodchips can impart a desirable flavor characteristic that is not found in beers brewed using normal methods. Ideally, the woodchips will be from oak. They are normally toasted and can then be soaked in whisky, brandy, or any other liquor that you feel brave enough to try. You will need to soak the woodchips for at least 2 weeks prior to brewing. The woodchips can be added directly to the hot wort and then removed with the trub.

Beer-flavoring orange peel

25

The Basic Method

Ultimately, producing beer from a full mash requires care and skill, which will come with time and patience. Homebrewing with the all-grain method can potentially produce the best beer that you've ever tasted.

The Mash

1 Heat 20 litres/4½ gallons/5 US gallons of water to 72–75°C (162–167°F) in your boiler.

2 Weigh the malt and other constituents of the "grain grist" or mash roll ready for putting in the mash tun.

3 Use a large measuring jug to remove 10 litres/2¼ gallons/2½ US gallons of the boiler water for pouring into the mash tun.

4 Pour the water into the mash tun to warm it up and use a thermometer to check that the water is at a temperature of 72–75°C (162–167°F). Add hot or cold water to adjust the temperature as necessary.

5 Add the grain grist to the water in the mash tun. Stir the grain grist gently into the water, making sure that there are no dry lumps of grain, until you have a porridge-like substance.

6 After stirring, the temperature should fall to 65–68°C (149–154°F). Allow to stand, covered, for 60–90 minutes (see individual recipes for the mashing time.)

7 Drain the mash tun slowly into a bucket or fermenting bin for 10 minutes. Don't allow it to run dry or you will end up with a set mash. Pour this back in and repeat.

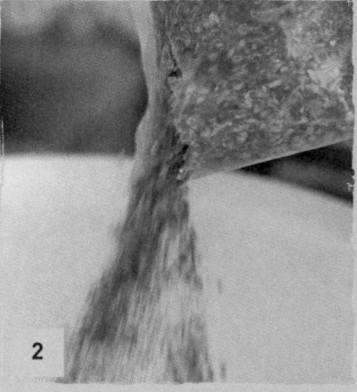

2

3

4

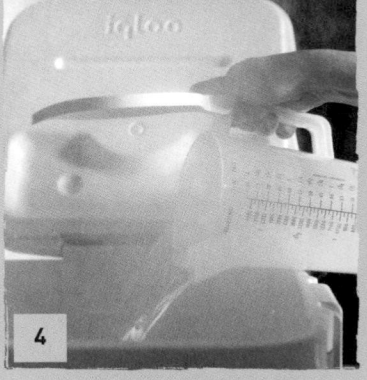

5

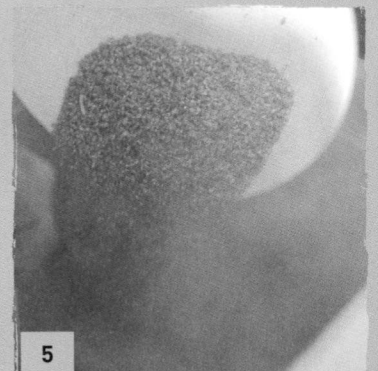

7

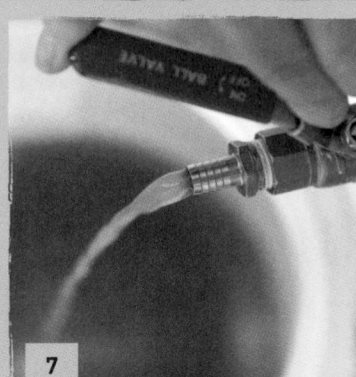

7

The Sparge

8 Pour the wort into a watering can ready for sparging. Start the sparge with about the same amount of water that you used for the mash (i.e. 10 litres/ 2¼ gallons/2½ US gallons) at a temperature of 75–80°C (167–175°F).

9 When sparging, go slowly and don't allow water to sit on top of the grain. Let it all drain through before adding the next load, leaving 10–15 minutes between each sparge. Repeat as necessary. Remember, you will need approximately the same amount of water for the sparge as you did for the mash. This will be your brewing wort.

The Boil

10 Place the hop strainer in the boiler to create your copper before transferring the wort. If you don't, the tap will get blocked with hops and removing it will stir cloudy proteins around your beer. Transfer the wort into the copper and turn up the heat until it comes to the boil.

11 Now chuck in your bittering hops (see page 24) and be as rough as you like with the stirring. Don't forget to take in a draw on that aroma. Keep the heat at a rolling boil (not a simmer) for an hour or so.

12 Throw in your finings (usually 5 minutes from the end of the boil) to "drop" your beer "bright" according to the manufacturer's instructions. Brewers use isinglass/ sturgeon fish gut, which acts as a magnet to pull cloud-creating particles down to the

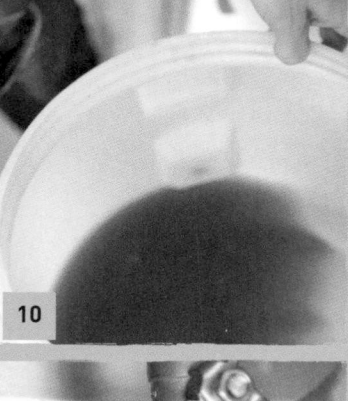

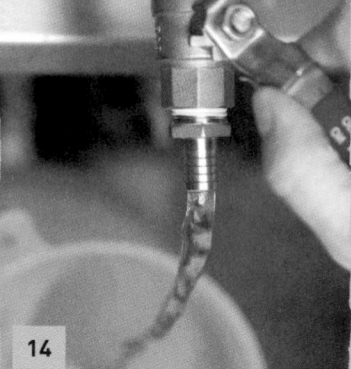

bottom, thus "dropping" the beer "bright" and clear. Irish moss, which is derived from seaweed, is the most common choice of fining, while Protofloc is a popular brand. Gelatin is also used by some brewers. All these finings are available online or from a local homebrew store. Isinglass may be obtainable, as might yeast, from your local microbrewery or good real-ale pub.

13 Turn off the heat and add the aroma hops after 5–10 minutes. Stir and leave to soak. After 20 minutes, stir again and repeat once more after another 20 minutes or so.

14 If you haven't been clean so far, now you have to be! Drain the copper to allow the hopped wort infusion to flow into the fermenting bin, or carboy, leaving behind the strained hops that haven't blocked your tap (you clever thing you!)

15 Adjust the volume to 23 litres/ 5 gallons/6 US gallons with cold water, then cover, and cool to about 20°C (68°F). This can be done in a bath filled with ice-laden water or with a cooling element from a homebrew store. Carboys are great if you are planning to bottle your beer because they save time by allowing you to add priming sugar in one go, rather than individually to each bottle. They also allow you to see clearly how well the yeast is performing.

Fermentation

16 Use a sterilized container to mix the yeast with some sterile water or wort, ready for pitching it into the fermenter. You can store any remaining yeast in the fridge for your next brew (but for no longer than a week.)

17 When the wort is at 20°C (68°F), pitch your chosen yeast to ferment. Whatever yeast you use, it is vital to get it going well to prevent any possible infection, so give the wort a good rouse or stir to introduce oxygen to the beer and assist the yeast's consumption of those lovely fermentable sugars.

18 Ideally, check the original gravity of the wort with a hydrometer at 20°C (68°F).

Hydrometers are calibrated at this temperature, so check you are reading 20°C (68°F).

19 Now cover the fermenter with its sterilized lid, bung and airlock, and then store at 18–20°C (65–68°F) to ensure proper fermentation.

20 After 3–5 days, check and record the original gravity with the hydrometer. This will help you spot if things aren't going to plan. A good hydrometer will have a useful little colored band to help you identify when the gravity has fallen to around 1010, thus telling you that it is time to rack your beer. Alternatively, when the gravity has remained static for 2 consecutive days, it is usually done – this will be the final gravity. Bang tidy!

16

How to use the Recipes in this Book

ORIGINAL GRAVITY	1047
	(This refers to the weight of the beer before fermentation)
WATER	23 litres/5 gallons/6 US gallons
	(The amount of water that you will need for mashing and sparging)

MASH ROLL	WEIGHT
Pale ale malt	4.9kg (10¾ lb)
Crystal malt	200g (7oz)
Chocolate malt	45g (1½ oz)

(The mixture of grains required to make up the "grain bill" or "mash roll" for mashing)

MASH SCHEDULE	1 hour
	(The amount of time you will need to leave your mash roll in the mash tun)

IN THE BOIL	WEIGHT	TIME
UK Challenger	22g (¾ oz)	90 minutes
UK Bramling Cross	20g (¾ oz)	20 minutes from end
UK Fuggles	16g (½ oz)	5 minutes from end
Protofloc/Irish moss	1 teaspoon	15 minutes from end

(Provides the list of hop types, adjuncts, and finings you will need to boil up in the brewing wort)

BOIL DURATION	1½ hours
	(The amount of time for which you will need to boil the hops and other ingredients in the brewing wort)
YEAST	London ale yeast – WY-1318
	(Provides the amount and recommended type of yeast for the particular beer)
TARGET FG	1012
	(This is the final gravity and refers to the weight of the beer after fermentation)
TARGET ABV	4.6%
	(Indicates the alcoholic strength of the beer)

A Little More Brew Science

Although homebrewing beer is essentially a simple, step-by-step process, there is a certain amount of science involved in it. Although you may think that the scientific explanations will be rather dull, reading through this next section should give you the knowledge to make your homebrewing more interesting.

Water

Before you start experimenting with this, it is worth contacting your local water board and requesting a full alkalinity analysis of your water in ppm (parts per million.) In general, calcium carbonate is added to make dark beer from soft water and to help balance the roasted grain's natural acidity, whereas calcium chloride and calcium sulphate (gypsum) are used to lower the pH and thereby increase acidity. Most water supplies have too much carbonate and not enough calcium for brewing pale ales and bitter.

Brupaks' CRS (Carbonate Reducing Solution) and DLS (Dry Liquor Salts) are great products but, as with most things, there is an endless supply of products available that perform the same function. For lager, some recommend using CRS in the mash liquor with lactic acid added to the mash tun to lower the pH. For the purist, a specialist German acid malt can be added to the grist to achieve the same effect.

Yeasts—culturing and rehydration

Yeast is the lowest form of plant life, but it does have at least one useful function—the creation of alcohol. The main objective is to ensure that the brewing wort is colonized quickly by enough strong yeast cells, which drastically reduces the risk of infection. Hence, you need to plan your yeast ahead of brewing to ensure that it gets off to a good start.

A low pitching rate will give a slow fermentation, thus increasing the competition from bacteria and wild yeasts. It will also lead to higher diacetyl levels (diacetyls are a natural by-product of fermentation) and possibly pediococcus infection, the latter of which is, of course, no fun. A high pitching rate will decrease the pH and reduce bacterial growth just as it will the formation of diacetyl. A word here on diacetyl: in strict moderation, diacetyl is not harmful to your beer and its presence is, in fact, relatively acceptable in some beers, particularly more flavorsome ales. This is not a universally shared opinion, however, and some brewers consider it a hindrance to their beer in spite of the occasionally positive flavor it imparts.

THE YEAST BANK

The Brewing Industry Research Center, in Nutfield, Surrey acts as the United Kingdom's yeast bank. Yep, that's right; all commercial brewers deposit strains of their yeast here for safe-keeping and posterity. This is how Westerham Brewery was able to secure the original Black Eagle Brewery yeast that hadn't been used since it closed in 1965.

HOP TABLE

Hop Name	AA Range	Substitutions
Admiral (UK)	13.5–16%	Target, Northdown, Challenger
Ahtanum (US)	7–9%	Cascade, Amarillo
Amarillo Gold (US)	6–9%	Cascade, Centennial
Apollo (US)	18–22%	Centennial, Columbus, Amarillo
Blitzen (GR)	11–15%	Horizon, Magnum
Brambling Cross (UK)	5–8%	N/A
Bravo (US)	14–17%	Nugget
Brewer's Gold (UK)	6–8%	N. Brewer, Galena, Eroica,
Bullion (UK)	6–9%	German Chinook, Eroica, Brewer's Gold
Cascade (US)	4.5–7%	Centennial, Amarillo, Columbus
Centennial (US)	9–12%	Galena, Cascade, Columbus
Challenger (UK)	6.5–8.5%	Perle, N. Brewer
Chinook (US)	11–13%	Galena, Columbus, Target
Citra	10–12%	Cascade, Centennial, Ahtanum
Cluster (US)	5.5–8.5%	Eroica, Galena
Columbia (UK)	5.5%	Fuggles, Willamette
Columbus (Tomahawk) (US)	10–16%	Centennial, Nugget, Chinook
Comet (US)	9.5%	N/A
Crystal (US)	2–4.5%	Hersbrucker, Mt. Hood, Liberty
Eroica (US)	9–13%	Galena, N. Brewer, Nugget
First Gold (UK)	6.5–8.5%	ESB EKG, Crystal
Fuggles (UK)	4–5.5%	EKG, US Fuggles, Willamette
Fuggles (US)	4–5.5%	UK Fuggles, Willamette
Galena (US)	10–14%	Eroica, N. Brewer, Cluster, Chinook, Nugget
Glacier (US)	5–9%	Willamette, Fuggles, Goldings,
Goldings, East Kent (EKG)(UK)	4–6%	Fuggles, US Goldings
Goldings (US)	4–6%	EKG, Fuggles, Whitbread, Progress
Green Bullet (NZ)	13.5%	Styrian Goldings
Hallertauer (GR)	3–5%	Crystal, Liberty, Mittelfrueh
Hallertauer (US)	3.5–5.5%	Liberty, Ultra, Hallertauer (GR)
Hallertauer, Hersbrucker (GR)	1.5–5.5%	Mt. Hood, Liberty, Mittelfrueh
Hallertauer, Mittelfrueh (GR)	3–5.5%	Hallertauer, Mt. Hood, Liberty,
Hallertauer (NZ)	8.5%	Hallertauer, Mittelfrueh
Herald (UK)	12%	High-alpha English hops
Horizon (US)	11–14%	Magnum
Independent (US)	6%	Lagers N/A
Liberty (US)	3–6%	Mittlefrueh, Mt. Hood, Crystal
Lublin (Poland)	3–5%	Saaz, Tettnanger
Magnum (GR)	13–15%	Horizon
Magnum (US)	13–15%	Willamette, Fuggles, EKG.
Mt. Hood (US)	3–8%	Hersbrucker, Liberty, Crystal
Mt. Rainier (US)	6–8%	Hallertauer, Fuggles
Nelson Sauvin (NZ)	11–13%	N/A
Newport (US)	11.5–17%	Galena, Nugget, Fuggles, Magnum, Brewer's Gold

Hop Name	AA Range	Substitutions
Northdown (UK)	7.5–9.5%	N. Brewer
Northern Brewer (GR)	8–10%	Hallertauer, Mittelfrueh, Nugget
Nugget (US)	9–13%	Columbus, Target, Galena
Orion (GR)	7–9%	Perle
Pacific Gem (NZ)	15%	Bullion
Palisade (US)	5.5–9.5%	Willamette, Goldings
Perle (GR)	5–9%	Chinook, Galena, N. Brewer
Phoenix (UK)	4–8%	Challenger, EKG, Northdown
Pilgrim (UK)	11–13%	N/A
Pioneer (UK)	8–10%	EKG
Pride of Ringwood (AUS)	7–10%	Cluster, Galena
Primiant (Czech)	7–9%	N/A
Progress (UK)	6–8%	Fuggles, EKG
Revolution (US)	5%	N/A
Riwaka (NZ)	5–7%	Cascade, Centennial
Saaz (Czech)	3–4.5%	Tettnanger, Lublin, US Saaz
Saaz (US)	3–5%	Czech Saaz, Tettnanger
Santiam (US)	5–8%	Tettnanger, Spalt, Select Spalt
Saphir (GR)	4%	N/A
Select Spalt (GR)	4–6%	Spalt, Saaz, Tettnanger
Simcoe (US)	12–14%	N/A
Slovenian Celeia (Slovenia)	3–6%	Saaz, Styrian Goldings
Sorachi Ace (Japan)	13–16%	N/A
Southern Cross (NZ)	13%	N/A
Sovereign (UK)	4–6%	N/A
Spalt (GR)	4–6%	Saaz, Tettnanger, Select Spalt
Sterling (US)	6–9%	Saaz, Lublin
Sticklebract (NZ)	13–15%	N. Brewer
Strisselspalt (FR)	2–4%	Mt. Hood Crystal, Hersbrucker
Styrian Aurora (Slovenia)	7–9%	N. Brewer, Styrian Goldings
Styrian Goldings (Slovenia)	4–6%	Fuggles, Willamette
Summit (US)	17–19%	Simcoe, Amarillo
Sun (US)	14%	High-alpha US hops
Super Alpha (NZ)	13%	N/A
Target (UK)	9.5–12.5%	EKG, Fuggles, Willamette
Tettnang (GR)	3.5–5.5%	Saaz, Spalt, Tettnanger
Tradition (GR)	5–7%	Mittelfrueh, Liberty, Ultra
Ultra (US)	2–4%	Liberty, Hallertauer, Saaz
Vanguard (US)	5–7%	Hallertauer Mittelfrueh, Saaz
Warrior (US)	14–17%	Nugget
Whitbread Golding Variety (UK)	5–7%	EKG, Progress
Willamette (US)	4–6%	Fuggles, EKG, Tett., Sty., Goldings
Yakima Golding (US)	5%	EKG, Progress, Fuggles
Zeus (US)	13–17%	Other high alpha hops

Before the yeast cells can go forth and multiply, they will have to be rehydrated to replace the water they lost when they were dried out. As yeasts are living organisms, the rehydration temperature is critical for a good fermenting performance. Your objective here is to reduce the lag phase (the time necessary for the yeasts to start fermenting sugars to alcohol after you have pitched/inoculated the brewing wort). Guaranteed success on this front can be achieved by rehydrating the yeast at a higher temperature than the initial fermentation temperature.

Top-fermenting ale yeasts should be rehydrated at a temperature of 25–29°C (77–84°F) and bottom-fermenting lager yeasts at a temperature range of 21–25°C (70–77°F). For dry yeast like Fermentis, rehydrate by sprinkling the yeast into ten times its own weight of sterile water or wort. Gently stir and leave for 30 minutes, then pitch the resultant cream into the fermentation vessel. Remember to rouse (or stir) first.

Pale lager

CULTURE FROM BOTTLE There are a multitude of yeasts available to the homebrewer. If, however, you need one that is commercially unavailable, it's possible to culture a yeast from a bottle-conditioned beer. Unfortunately, the majority of commercial beers are not only filtered but also flash-pasteurized before bottling and so leave little or no yeast trace at all. However, a few brewers will bottle-condition their beers. To be sure if a bottle of beer is suitable, look out for a sediment at the bottom of the bottle when it is held up to the light.

Also bear in mind that commercial brewers will sometimes use two or three different yeasts in a batch of beer. Some of the yeast will be stronger than the others and so you will not necessarily be able to produce the same yeast strain even if you do culture them from the bottle. However, here is how to culture the yeast from a bottle:

1 Thoroughly clean all the equipment during this process. (You'll need to be even more thorough than if you were making a normal batch of beer.)
2 Make a wort with a specific gravity of 1015–1020.
3 Add a pinch of yeast nutrient to the wort.
4 Provide the yeast with carbohydrates, oxygen, and nutrients, remembering to feed the fragile yeast with only a little wort at a time.
5 Leaving the bottle cap on, wipe over the neck of the bottle and cap with a sanitizing solution, being careful not to disturb the sediment.
6 Pour off the beer and, again, make sure that you don't disturb the sediment.
7 Let the bottle warm up to room temperature, covering the opening with some sanitized aluminum (aluminium) foil.
8 Pour wort down the side of the bottle onto the yeast (using enough to cover the bottom) and swirl it around a little. Replace the aluminum foil.
9 Leave for between 1 to 3 days at a temperature of 70–90°F (21–32°C)—on top of a kitchen cupboard out of direct light will be sufficient.
10 Once signs of fermentation appear (i.e. cloudiness or frothing), transfer the fermenting wort into a small amount of fresh wort (approx. 1 tablespoon).
11 To get enough for a 23-litre-/5-gallon-/6-US-gallon batch, you will need to keep adding the wort in small stages until you have 1.5 litres (51 fl oz). Note that you are feeding the yeast, not drowning it!

CULTURE FROM UNSETTLED CASK Ideally, take a sample from a fresh unsettled barrel of beer. Make up a couple of pints of DME (dry malt extract), so that when you add a pint of the beer the original gravity is 1040ish. I use a demijohn and mag stirrer, and it can take a few days before results can be seen! Don't use the yeast culture if you don't get enough activity.

Fermentation Temperature Chart	Start Temperature	Top Temperature	Diacetyl Rest Temperature	Chill Temperature
ALE	18–20°C (65–68°F)	21–23°C (70–73°F)	Decrease from 20°C (68°F) to 16–17°C (61–63°F) for 24 hours	1–5°C (34–41°F) for chilled and filtered ale 0–12°C (32–54°F) for cask ale
LAGER	12°C (54°F)	15°C (60°F)	15°C (60°F) for 24–48 hours	1–3°C (34–37°F)

Temperature during fermentation

Firstly, always refer to the product packaging or specification sheets. Next, remember that the warmer the temperature at the beginning of the fermentation, the faster the fermentation will start, which will also increase the ester (a flavor compound created during fermentation) and diacetyl levels. So, it is important to regulate top temperatures, but be mindful that for the reabsorption of diacetyl you may have to allow the temperature to rise at the end of fermentation. Diacetyl absorption by the yeast is a good thing (it removes the errant diacetyl from running freely around your beer) and, occasionally, a gentle rise in temperatures can be employed at the end of the fermentation process to achieve good yeast flocculation (removal of sediment from a fluid) and better absorption of diaceytl.

Oxygenating the wort

Aerating your cooled wort immediately before pitching is essential for getting a good start with the fermentation. This can be achieved by rousing (or stirring), aeration, or direct oxygen injection. Whichever method you use, it is crucial that good hygiene is observed at all times. Best practice for the homebrewer is to get an aqua pump with micron filters to clean the air passing through. Aerating after pitching should only be performed during the first 12 hours because adding oxygen during late fermentation will increase the aldehyde levels and amplify diacetyl.

A note on beer replicas

Without wanting to demean the efforts of others, who have written extensively on the subject, you simply will not be able to reproduce a beer exactly. You cannot know all the techniques a brewer uses when designing a beer or all the components and variations of his mash. You will also be brewing with vastly different equipment. Many brewers use a different type of yeast for their bottled beer to that of keg or cask—not just to make it harder to obtain, but also to ensure preservation in the bottle.

It is, however, possible to get close and great fun to try. Bear in mind that many beer recipes of the same style often only vary in the grain bill by 56g (2oz) here or there. The grains are predominately the same.

Research is key to creating a reliable copy. Buy a bottle or can and check out the label and the brewers website for hints as to the type of hops and grains used. They will all tell you the ABV (alcohol by volume) and some the OG (original gravity). When you have all this information, compare the color to the EBC chart (see page 20). You can now employ the best cheating service a man has ever selflessly employed for the good of other brewers—Graham Wheeler's excellent "Beer Engine" program for Windows Xp, which is a free download. Simply punch in all your ingredients, the ABV, estimated IBU (International Bittering Units,) and EBC (European Brewing Convention), and the program will work out the weight of grain and hops required. Easy—well, not quite. You will still need to adjust and tweak the recipe once brewed to make it an acceptable copy—add sugars, subtract hops, lighten the grain, add the odd adjunct for head retention; and it may take a few attempts to get it right.

To convert SRM (Standard Research Method) to EBC:
(SRM x 2.65) - 1.2 = EBC.

To convert EBC to SRM:
(EBC x 0.375) + 0.46 = SRM.

33

Troubleshooting for Beerheads

WHY IS MY BEER FLAT?

Carbonating beer naturally with an active yeast can be tricky and it may take a couple of attempts to get a foamy head to your liking. If the beer is flat, then try using a couple more grams of bottling sugar or add 28g (1oz) of flaked wheat to the mash.

WHY IS MY BEER THIN AND WATERY?

This shows that not enough proteins were produced from the mash (proteins give the beer body). Try using 28–56g (1–2oz) of protein-rich wheat, and then mash hotter and shorter to achieve a much richer wort.

WHY HAS MY BEER BECOME THICK AND JELLY-LIKE?

Chuck it! This beer has a major infection. Acetobater and Pediococcus bacteria are present and have produced a polysaccharide goo. Reread the sanitizing section and sanitize better.

IS MY BEER SAFE TO DRINK IF IT SMELLS OF OLD SOCKS/CHEESE?

I wouldn't drink this beer if you offered it to me. Although it won't do you any harm, it is not going to taste good. This has happened because stale hops were used. Hops should smell sharp and fresh, not stale or musty. The solution is to store your hops in air-tight containers or even freeze any leftover hops for the next brew.

WHY DOES MY BEER LOOK HAZY?

This will not spoil the taste, but, aesthetically, it isn't pleasing after all that hard work. The reason the beer is hazy is that the proteins did not settle out and re-suspended during the chilling process. This also may have happened because of over-priming the bottles. Another reason is that the malt used may have been moldy. So, make sure your sanitizing is really top-notch, ensure the malt is within date and not moldy, and also check you are not over-priming the bottles.

WHY DOES MY BEER SMELL LIKE ROTTEN EGGS?

This could be one of two things: infection or the brew is just too long (especially if it is a lager). To solve this, leave the brew (if lager) for another week and see if the smell dissipates. If it doesn't, then it's an infection and is down to poor sanitizing. Obviously, throw any infected brew down the drain.

WHY DOES MY BEER SMELL LIKE A BARNYARD?

The hop molecules have been hit by certain light waves, which have broken them apart. Then, the pieces have combined with hydrogen sulphide to produce the awful smell. Beer must be bottled in brown glass and stored out of direct light.

WHY DOES MY BEER FROTH OVER WHEN I OPEN THE BOTTLE?

This is a classic sign that your brew has been infected with a wild yeast. However, if none of the normal sourness associated with wild yeast is present, then you could have simply over-primed the bottles. Take extra care over your sanitizing techniques or, if the latter is suspected, just tone down the level of priming sugar used. I would also suggest checking your malt is not moldy.

ENJOY!

If you are bored with the beers available commercially, then homebrewing is an option. Don't be put off if you are unsuccessful on your first attempt. Remember, practice really will make perfect and it happens to us all. In homebrewing circles, you are in good company, so let's get to work!

35

A WORD TO THE WISE

Every monastery used to brew its own beer for the monks and also for visitors. Today, only a few monasteries still brew beer, although commercial brewers make beers with monastic connections.

CHAPTER 1
BELGIAN BEERS

PATERS BEER

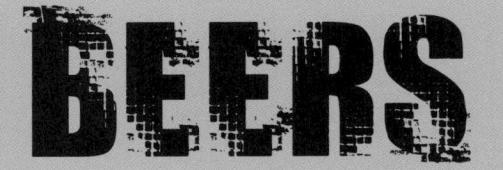

This is a type of Trappist beer, which, as the name suggests, originated from a Cistercian monastery in La Trappe, in Soligny, France. Although the Trappist monks were sworn to a life of strict asceticism, they were eventually allowed to brew beer. Paters beer or "father's beer" is a Trappist beer variety that was initially only meant for the monks themselves to drink. All Trappist beers are ales that are top-fermented and bottle-conditioned.

ORIGINAL GRAVITY	1085	
WATER	23 litres/5 gallons/6 US gallons	
MASH ROLL	WEIGHT	
Pale malt	3.85kg (8½lb)	
Munich malt	453g (1lb)	
Crystal malt	226g (8oz)	
Black malt	28g (1oz)	
MASH SCHEDULE	1 hour	
IN THE BOIL	WEIGHT	TIME
Dark brown sugar	453g (1lb)	90 minutes
Honey	226g (8oz)	at the end of the boil
Hallertauer	56g (2oz)	60 minutes from end
UK Goldings	28g (1oz)	60 minutes from end
Protofloc	1 teaspoon	15 minutes from end
BOIL DURATION	1½ hours	
YEAST	Trappist ale yeast—WLP-500	
TARGET FG	1018	
TARGET ABV	8%	

37

ABBEY BEER

As the name indicates, Abbey Beer is a monastic style of beer. In this recipe, I have developed my own version of an abbey beer for you to sample. There are in total 18 certified commercial producers of this style of beer in existence today; that is to say, this is not a rigid style of brewing. However, you will usually find that most monastic-style beers are distinctive and made to an exceptionally high standard.

ORIGINAL GRAVITY	1062	
WATER	23 litres/5 gallons/6 US gallons	
MASH ROLL	**WEIGHT**	
Pilsner malt	4.8kg (10½lb)	
Munich malt	453g (1lb)	
Chocolate malt	28g (1oz)	
MASH SCHEDULE	1 hour	
IN THE BOIL	**WEIGHT**	**TIME**
Willamette	28g (1oz)	60 minutes
Fuggles	28g (1oz)	15 minutes from end
Protofloc	1 teaspoon	15 minutes from end
BOIL DURATION	1 hour	
YEAST	Belgian Abbey—WY-1214	
TARGET FG	1008	
TARGET ABV	4.6%	

A WORD TO THE WISE

For all the recipes in this book, no starter yeast is required. You simply need to use Wyeast labs smack-packs.

 AMBER ALE

Amber in name, amber in color. This is a great beer to serve with pasta covered in shavings of Parmesan cheese.

ORIGINAL GRAVITY	1080	
WATER	23 litres/5 gallons/6 US gallons	
MASH ROLL	WEIGHT	
Dark Munich malt	5.4kg (12lb)	
Dextrose (corn sugar)	970g (2lb)	
MASH SCHEDULE	1 hour	
IN THE BOIL	WEIGHT	TIME
Northern Brewer	28g (1oz)	60 minutes
Protofloc	1 teaspoon	15 minutes from end
BOIL DURATION	1 hour	
YEAST	Belgian—WY-3522	
TARGET FG	1020	
TARGET ABV	5.3%	

 GOLDEN ALE

This beer is light in color and taste, making it a perfect drink to accompany an afternoon in the sun.

ORIGINAL GRAVITY	1073	
WATER	23 litres/5 gallons/6 US gallons	
MASH ROLL	WEIGHT	
Pilsner malt	4.9kg (11lb)	
Dextrose (corn sugar)	907g (2lb)	
Torrified wheat	226g (8oz)	
Honey	226g (8oz)	
MASH SCHEDULE	1 hour	
IN THE BOIL	WEIGHT	TIME
Hallertauer	15g (1/2oz)	60 minutes
Styrian Goldings	31g (1oz)	60 minutes
Hallertauer	15g (1/2oz)	30 minutes from end
Saaz	15g (1/2oz)	30 minutes from end
Styrian Goldings	31g (1oz)	30 minutes from end
Saaz	15g (1/2oz)	1 minute from end
Protofloc	1 teaspoon	15 minutes from end
BOIL DURATION	1 hour	
YEAST	Belgian Ardennes—WY-3522	
TARGET FG	1010	
TARGET ABV	8.4%	

41

BLONDE ALE

This ale has a fantastic, deep golden color that sets off the creamy white head to great effect.

ORIGINAL GRAVITY	1050	
WATER	23 litres/5 gallons/6 US gallons	
MASH ROLL	**WEIGHT**	
Pale malt	4.3kg (9½lb)	
Light crystal malt	453g (1lb)	
Carapils	113g (4oz)	
Caramalt	113g (4oz)	
MASH SCHEDULE	1 hour	
IN THE BOIL	**WEIGHT**	**TIME**
Perle	31g (1oz)	60 minutes
Cascade	28g (1oz)	10 minutes from end
Protofloc	1 teaspoon	15 minutes from end
BOIL DURATION	1 hour	
YEAST	American ale—WY-1056	
TARGET FG	1012	
TARGET ABV	4.98%	

ELDERFLOWER BLOND

With its high hopping rate and the elderflowers, this is a refreshing, aromatic summer ale.

ORIGINAL GRAVITY	1073	
WATER	23 litres/5 gallons/6 US gallons	
MASH ROLL	**WEIGHT**	
2-row pale malt	4.3kg (9½lb)	
Munich malt	453g (1lb)	
Carapils	453g (1lb)	
Torrified wheat	226g (8oz)	
MASH SCHEDULE	1 hour	
IN THE BOIL	**WEIGHT**	**TIME**
Hallertauer	35g (1¼oz)	60 minutes
Saaz	28g (1oz)	10 minutes from end
Fresh or dried elderflowers	200g (7oz)	at flame-out
Protofloc	1 teaspoon	15 minutes from end
BOIL DURATION	1 hour	
YEAST	Belgian Ardennes—WY-3522	
TARGET FG	1010	
TARGET ABV	5.5%	

A WORD TO THE WISE

In Blonde Ale, depending on the hops used, you are aiming for an earthy hop nose with a lightly sweet Pils malt character.

43

A WORD TO THE WISE

The use of the Nelson Sauvin hop is optional, but does add a special edge to this brew.

CHAMPAGNE BEER

This is essentially a beer that is brewed in the normal way, but then fermented with Champagne yeast. The original Champagne beer would have been trippel-matured with Champagne yeast and then aged in Champagne caves with the bottles at an angle so that the yeast could collect in the necks before being frozen and removed. This beer makes a great aperitif and can easily become a favorite among those who do not really like beer.

ORIGINAL GRAVITY	1082	
WATER	23 litres/5 gallons/6 US gallons	
MASH ROLL	WEIGHT	
Pilsner malt	3.35kg (7^1/$_4$lb)	
2-row pale malt	1.7kg (3^3/$_4$lb)	
Carapils	335g (11^3/$_4$oz)	
Rye malt	335g (11^3/$_4$oz)	
Belgian light candi sugar	1kg (2^1/$_4$lb)	
MASH SCHEDULE	1 hour	
IN THE BOIL	WEIGHT	TIME
Fuggles	38g (1^1/$_4$lb)	60 minutes
Hellertauer	21g (^{3}/$_4$oz)	60 minutes
Nelson Sauvin	10g (^{1}/$_4$oz)	5 minutes from end
Saaz	19g (^{3}/$_4$oz)	1 minute from end
Protofloc	1 teaspoon	15 minutes from end
BOIL DURATION	1 hour	
YEAST	Pasteur Champagne—WY-4021	
EXPECTED FG	1016	
EXPECTED ABV	4.7%	

DUBBEL

Belgian brewers are renowned for their ability to create great beers. Considering the complexity of the flavors in Belgian beer, you would be forgiven for thinking they were alchemists but, traditionally, these brews were created in monasteries because the monks were able to obtain ingredients from around the world.

ORIGINAL GRAVITY	1060	
WATER	23 litres/5 gallons/6 US gallons	
MASH ROLL	WEIGHT	
Belgian Pilsener malt	4.9kg (11lb)	
Belgian biscuit malt	341g (12oz)	
Belgian aromatic malt	264g (9¼oz)	
Caramunich	34g (1¼oz)	
Belgian special B	11g (¼oz)	
MASH SCHEDULE	1 hour	
IN THE BOIL	WEIGHT	TIME
Belgian candi sugar amber	600g (1¼lb)	90 minutes
Styrian Aurora	24g (¾oz)	60 minutes from end
Czech Saaz	10g (¼oz)	15 minutes from end
Protofloc	1 teaspoon	15 minutes from end
BOIL DURATION	1½ hours	
YEAST	Belgian Abbey—WY-1214	
TARGET FG	1010	
TARGET ABV	6.6%	

"Always do sober what you said you'd do drunk. That will teach you to keep your mouth shut."
ERNEST HEMINGWAY (1899-1961)

▶ TRIPPEL

The hops in this beer create a spicy, clove-like aroma with a rounded malt flavor, masking the high alcohol content.

ORIGINAL GRAVITY	1082	
WATER	23 litres/5 gallons/6 US gallons	
MASH ROLL	WEIGHT	
Pilsner malt	3.35kg (7¼lb)	
2-row pale malt	1.7kg (3¾lb)	
Carapils	335g (11¾oz)	
Rye malt	335g (11¾oz)	
Belgian light candi sugar	1kg (2¼lb)	
MASH SCHEDULE	1 hour	
IN THE BOIL	WEIGHT	TIME
UK Goldings	38g (1¼oz)	60 minutes
Hellertauer	21g (¾oz)	60 minutes
Saaz	19g (¾oz)	1 minute from end
Protofloc	1 teaspoon	15 minutes from end
BOIL DURATION	1 hour	
YEAST	Belgian Abbey—WY-1214	
EXPECTED FG	1016	
EXPECTED ABV	7.5%	

QUADDRUPPEL

This style of beer is the strongest, richest, and most complex in flavor of all the Belgian beers.

ORIGINAL GRAVITY	1084	
WATER	23 litres/5 gallons/6 US gallons	
MASH ROLL	WEIGHT	
Maris otter	6.3kg (13¾lb)	
Dark Munich malt	453g (1lb)	
Belgian dark candi sugar	453g (1lb)	
Dark brown sugar	340g (12oz)	
Light brown sugar	340g (12oz)	
Caramunich III	113g (4oz)	
Belgian special B	28g (1oz)	
MASH SCHEDULE	1½ hours	
IN THE BOIL	WEIGHT	TIME
Saaz	28g (1oz)	60 minutes
Perle	28g (1oz)	15 minutes from end
Peppercorns (crushed)	1 teaspoon	20 minutes from end
Protofloc	1 teaspoon	15 minutes from end
BOIL DURATION	1 hour	
YEAST	Belgian Abbey ale—WY-1762	
TARGET FG	1015	
TARGET ABV	9.2%	

A WORD TO THE WISE

The hops in Trippel Beer are there, ultimately, to balance the sweetness of the malts.

RED BEER

Strong on taste and alcohol, this beer contains a little chocolate malt, which gives it a smoky flavor.

ORIGINAL GRAVITY	1064	
WATER	23 litres/5 gallons/6 US gallons	
MASH ROLL	**WEIGHT**	
Maris otter	4.9kg (11lb)	
Caramunich	226g (8oz)	
Aromatic malt	110g (3³/₄oz)	
Chocolate malt	28g (1oz)	
MASH SCHEDULE	1 hour	
IN THE BOIL	**WEIGHT**	**TIME**
Tettnanger	35g (1¹/₄oz)	60 minutes
Galena	14g (¹/₂oz)	15 minutes from end
Styrian Goldings	7g (¹/₄oz)	15 minutes from end
Candi sugar (light to medium in color)	453g (1lb)	near the end
Protofloc	1 teaspoon	15 minutes from end
BOIL DURATION	1 hour	
YEAST	Belgian ale—WY-1762	
TARGET FG	1015	
TARGET ABV	8%	

FLEMISH RED

Traditionally matured in oak casks, the roasted malts give this beer its distinctive, deep reddish brown hue.

ORIGINAL GRAVITY	1052	
WATER	23 litres/5 gallons/6 US gallons	
MASH ROLL	**WEIGHT**	
Vienna malt	3.6kg (8lb)	
Flaked maize	1.3kg (2³/₄lb)	
Caravienne	453g (1lb)	
Caramel Pilsner malt	453g (1lb)	
Belgian aromatic malt	453g (1lb)	
Belgian special B	85g (3oz)	
MASH SCHEDULE	1 hour	
IN THE BOIL	**WEIGHT**	**TIME**
Fuggles	28g (1oz)	75 minutes
UK Goldings	14g (¹/₂oz)	15 minutes from end
Protofloc	1 teaspoon	15 minutes from end
BOIL DURATION	1¹/₄ hours	
YEAST	Belgian ale—WY-1762	
TARGET FG	1012	
TARGET ABV	5.3%	

SAISON

This beer is a Flemish classic and its name simply means "season." Once brewed as a refreshment for Belgian farm workers as they gathered in the harvest in late summer, this brew originates from the Walloon, a French-speaking region of Belgium. As the flavor comes from the spices, citrus fruits, and herbs that are added at the boiling stage and not from the hops, many Belgian farmers would brew their own special version of the beer.

ORIGINAL GRAVITY	1049	
WATER	23 litres/5 gallons/6 US gallons	
MASH ROLL	WEIGHT	
Pilsner malt	3kg (6^{1}/$_{2}$lb)	
Vienna malt	1.1kg (2^{1}/$_{2}$lb)	
Torrified wheat	240g (8^{1}/$_{2}$oz)	
Medium crystal malt	210g (7^{1}/$_{4}$oz)	
Belgian aromatic malt	160g (5^{1}/$_{2}$oz)	
MASH SCHEDULE	1 hour	
IN THE BOIL	WEIGHT	TIME
German Brewers Gold	19g (³/$_{4}$oz)	90 minutes
UK Goldings	10g (¹/$_{4}$oz)	30 minutes from end
Slovenian Styrian Goldings	12g (¹/$_{2}$oz)	10 minutes from end
Star anise	10g (¹/$_{4}$oz)	20 minutes from end
Lemon zest	1 whole	10 minutes from end
Orange zest	2 whole	10 minutes from end
Coriander seeds (crushed)	20g (³/$_{4}$oz)	10 minutes from end
Freshly ground black pepper	1 teaspoon	5 minutes from end
Protofloc	1 teaspoon	15 minutes from end
BOIL DURATION	1^{1}/$_{2}$ hours	
YEAST	Belgian Saison—WY-3724	
TARGET FG	1009	
TARGET ABV	5.3%	

A WORD TO THE WISE

Try adding some cardamom pods to your Saison Beer during the boil.

54

A WORD TO THE WISE

For a delicious Christmas beer, try just adding 3 cinnamon sticks and 6 whole cloves with the hops and then boil as normal.

CHRISTMAS BEER

This is a specialty beer that is very strong, as well as full of spice and robust flavors. Every brewery will have its own take on a Christmas beer and you should be prepared to experiment with your own quantities of spices to achieve just the right taste for you. The recipe given here is meant to provide you with a guideline only, so be brave and try your hand at making something of your very own that's full of Christmas cheer.

ORIGINAL GRAVITY	1046	
WATER	23 litres/5 gallons/6 US gallons	
MASH ROLL	WEIGHT	
American 2-row pale malt	3.4kg (7½lb)	
Vienna malt	1.1kg (2½lb)	
Caramel malt	453g (1lb)	
Victory malt	453g (1lb)	
Caramunich	226g (8oz)	
Belgian dark candi sugar	226g (8oz)	
Honey malt	226g (8oz)	
Carafa I	113g (4oz)	
MASH SCHEDULE	1 hour	
IN THE BOIL	WEIGHT	TIME
Saaz	16g (½oz)	60 minutes
Hersbrucker	16g (½oz)	60 minutes
Styrian Goldings	14g (½oz)	60 minutes
Styrian Goldings	14g (½oz)	15 minutes from end
Hersbrucker	15g (½oz)	5 minutes from end
Star anise	10g (¼oz)	20 minutes from end
Cinnamon sticks	3	10 minutes from end
Whole cloves	7	10 minutes from end
Fresh root ginger (chopped)	30g (1oz)	10 minutes from end
Ground nutmeg	1 teaspoon	10 minutes from end
Protofloc	1 teaspoon	15 minutes from end
BOIL DURATION	1 hour	
YEAST	Belgian ale—WY-1762	
TARGET FG	1015	
TARGET ABV	7.3%	

55

WHEAT BEER

A traditional Flemish beer that does not depend solely on the hops to add flavor to the malt.

ORIGINAL GRAVITY	1046	
WATER	23 litres/5 gallons/6 US gallons	
MASH ROLL	WEIGHT	
Torrified wheat	2.48kg (5^1/$_2$lb)	
Pilsner malt	2.48kg (5^1/$_2$lb)	
MASH SCHEDULE	1 hour	
IN THE BOIL	WEIGHT	TIME
Fuggles	31g (1oz)	90 minutes
Orange zest (without pith)	15g (^{1}/$_2$oz)	15 minutes from end
Coriander seeds (crushed)	23g (^{3}/$_4$oz)	10 minutes from end
Cumin seeds	5g (^{1}/$_8$oz)	10 minutes from end
Protofloc	1 teaspoon	15 minutes from end
BOIL DURATION	1^1/$_2$ hours	
YEAST	Belgian wheat—WY-3942	
EXPECTED FG	1011	
EXPECTED ABV	4.6%	

SPICED ALE

A perfect beer for Christmas. You can add other spices such as a pinch of cinnamon to increase its complexity.

ORIGINAL GRAVITY	1048	
WATER	23 litres/5 gallons/6 US gallons	
MASH ROLL	WEIGHT	
English 2-row pale malt	4kg (8^3/$_4$lb)	
Medium crystal malt	210g (7^1/$_4$oz)	
Honey	600g (1^1/$_4$lb)	
MASH SCHEDULE	1^1/$_2$ hours	
IN THE BOIL	WEIGHT	TIME
Target	30g (1oz)	90 minutes
Hallertau Hersbruck	35g (1^1/$_4$oz)	10 minutes from end
Orange zest	35g (1^1/$_4$oz)	15 minutes from end
Fresh root ginger (chopped)	25g (^{3}/$_4$oz)	15 minutes from end
Protofloc	1 teaspoon	15 minutes from end
BOIL DURATION	1^1/$_2$ hours	
YEAST	Saison—WY-3711	
TARGET FG	1010	
TARGET ABV	4.8%	

"Drunk words are sober thoughts."
ANONYMOUS

WILDFLOWER WITBIER

When poured, this beer should have a well-rounded, golden color and a light sweet aroma.

ORIGINAL GRAVITY	1052	
WATER	23 litres/5 gallons/6 US gallons	

MASH ROLL	WEIGHT	
White wheat	2.23kg (5lb)	
2-row pale malt	1.8kg (4lb)	
Vienna malt	412g (14^{1}/$_{2}$oz)	
Flaked barley	110g (3^{3}/$_{4}$oz)	

MASH SCHEDULE	1 hour

IN THE BOIL	WEIGHT	TIME
Cascade	16g (^{1}/$_{2}$oz)	60 minutes
Cascade	16g (^{1}/$_{2}$oz)	10 minutes from end
Oranges	6	20 minutes from end
Grapefruit	1	20 minutes from end
Chamomile teabag	1	15 minutes from end
Coriander seeds (crushed)	1 teaspoon	10 minutes from end
Protofloc	1 teaspoon	15 minutes from end

BOIL DURATION	1 hour
YEAST	Belgian Witbier—WY-3944
TARGET FG	1009
TARGET ABV	5.2%

BLACKBERRY WITBIER

A beer with a subtle sweetness, the off-white head you get on pouring quickly disappears.

ORIGINAL GRAVITY	1040
WATER	23 litres/5 gallons/6 US gallons

MASH ROLL	WEIGHT
2-row pale malt	2.2kg (4^{3}/$_{4}$lb)
White wheat malt	2.2kg (4^{3}/$_{4}$lb)
Flaked oats	570g (1^{1}/$_{4}$lb)
Munich malt	113g (4oz)

MASH SCHEDULE	1^{1}/$_{2}$ hours

IN THE BOIL	WEIGHT	TIME
Goldings	28g (1oz)	60 minutes
Goldings	14g (^{1}/$_{2}$oz)	20 minutes from end
Protofloc	1 teaspoon	15 minutes from end
Blackberries	1.4kg (3lb)	at primary fermentation for 3 days

BOIL DURATION	1 hour
YEAST	Belgian Witbier—WY-3944
TARGET FG	1015
TARGET ABV	6.1%

 STOUT

Belgian Stout was first made by a small number of artisan brewers, but caught on in America where great stouts have been made.

ORIGINAL GRAVITY	1080	
WATER	23 litres/5 gallons/6 US gallons	
MASH ROLL	**WEIGHT**	
Pilsen malt	5.4kg (12lb)	
Munich malt	910g (2lb)	
Torrified wheat	453g (1lb)	
Chocolate malt	453g (1lb)	
Roast barley	453g (1lb)	
Belgian special B	453g (1lb)	
MASH SCHEDULE	1 hour	
IN THE BOIL	**WEIGHT**	**TIME**
Belgian dark candi syrup	453g (1lb)	90 minutes
Northern Brewer	28g (1oz)	60 minutes from end
Fuggles	28g (1oz)	30 minutes from end
Fuggles	12g (1/2oz)	at the end
Protofloc	1 teaspoon	15 minutes from end
BOIL DURATION	1 1/2 hours	
YEAST	Belgian Abbey II—WY-1762	
TARGET FG	1010	
TARGET ABV	7.5%	

 TAFELBIER

Literally meaning "table beer," weak Tafelbier was often found in Belgian school refectories up until the 1970s.

ORIGINAL GRAVITY	1023	
WATER	23 litres/5 gallons/6 US gallons	
MASH ROLL	**WEIGHT**	
Maris otter	1kg (2 1/4lb)	
Caravienne	453g (1lb)	
Torrified wheat	226g (8oz)	
Belgian aromatic malt	170g (6oz)	
Belgian light candi sugar	141g (5oz)	
MASH SCHEDULE	1 hour	
IN THE BOIL	**WEIGHT**	**TIME**
Tradition	10g (1/4oz)	60 minutes
Protofloc	1 teaspoon	15 minutes from end
BOIL DURATION	1 hour	
YEAST	Belgian ale—WY-1762	
TARGET FG	1004	
TARGET ABV	2.5%	

A WORD TO THE WISE

For stout, boil down the first runnings in order to caramelize.

A WORD TO THE WISE
For Bitter, try using Northern Brewer instead of Northdown as a hop variation.

CHAPTER 2

BRITISH BEERS

BITTER

This is the English term for pale ale. There are five variations in strength of bitter. It is most commonly sold as an ordinary Bitter (usually described as an IPA,) which generally has an ABV of up to 4.1%. Please note that IPA in America and elsewhere will be stronger. Best Bitter has an ABV of 4.2–4.7%, while the remaining three variations, referred to as Special Bitter, Extra Special Bitter, and Premium Bitter, have varying ABV percentages.

ORIGINAL GRAVITY	1037	
WATER	23 litres/5 gallons/6 US gallons	
MASH ROLL	WEIGHT	
Pale ale malt	3.65kg (8lb)	
Torrified wheat	265g (9¼oz)	
Medium crystal malt	100g (3½oz)	
Black malt	65g (2¼oz)	
MASH SCHEDULE	1 hour	
IN THE BOIL	WEIGHT	TIME
UK Northdown	20g (³⁄₄oz)	90 minutes
UK First Gold	10g (¼oz)	45 minutes from end
UK Bramling Cross	10g (¼oz)	10 minutes from end
Irish moss	1 teaspoon	15 minutes from end
BOIL DURATION	1½ hours	
YEAST	Safale—DCL-S04	
TARGET FG	1009	
TARGET ABV	3.9%	

BEST BITTER

Once the preferred choice of the working man, Best Bitter is a good starting-point for any aspiring homebrewer.

ORIGINAL GRAVITY	1047	
WATER	23 litres/5 gallons/6 US gallons	
MASH ROLL	WEIGHT	
Pale ale malt	4.9kg (10¾lb)	
Crystal malt	200g (7oz)	
Chocolate malt	45g (1½oz)	
MASH SCHEDULE	1 hour	
IN THE BOIL	WEIGHT	TIME
UK Challenger	22g (¾oz)	90 minutes
UK Bramling Cross	20g (¾oz)	20 minutes from end
UK Fuggles	16g (½oz)	5 minutes from end
Protofloc/Irish moss	1 teaspoon	15 minutes from end
BOIL DURATION	1½ hours	
YEAST	London ale—WY-1318	
TARGET FG	1012	
TARGET ABV	4.6%	

▶ EXTRA SPECIAL BITTER

An Extra Special Bitter usually uses British hops and has lots of malty, fruity flavor.

ORIGINAL GRAVITY	1053	
WATER	23 litres/5 gallons/6 US gallons	
MASH ROLL	WEIGHT	
Pale ale malt	4.93kg (10¾lb)	
Medium crystal malt	290g (10¼oz)	
Torrified wheat	210g (7¼oz)	
Chocolate malt	115g (4oz)	
MASH SCHEDULE	1 hour	
IN THE BOIL	WEIGHT	TIME
Light brown sugar	115g (4oz)	90 minutes
Williamette	19g (¾oz)	90 minutes
UK Bramling Cross	18g (½oz)	30 minutes from end
UK Goldings	13g (½oz)	30 minutes from end
UK Goldings	14g (½oz)	10 minutes from end
Protofloc	1 teaspoon	15 minutes from end
BOIL DURATION	1½ hours	
YEAST	British ale II—WY-1335	
TARGET FG	1013	
TARGET ABV	5.3%	

A WORD TO THE WISE

Extra Special Bitter is a little more bitter than its standard bitter counterparts and has a higher alcohol content. It is really more of a slow-and-savor kind of brew!

INDIA PALE ALE

A rather enterprising brewer from England decided during the British occupation of India to develop a beer that could mature on the boat journey rather than in a cellar back in England, thus making good use of the empty cargo ships on their return trip to India. This beer, known as IPA, became incredibly popular with the expats, which is easy to understand given its fantastic hoppy flavor and middling strength.

ORIGINAL GRAVITY	1052	
WATER	23 litres/5 gallons/6 US gallons	
MASH ROLL	WEIGHT	
Pale ale malt	5.25kg (11$\frac{1}{2}$lb)	
Medium crystal malt	420g (14$\frac{3}{4}$oz)	
MASH SCHEDULE	1 hour	
IN THE BOIL	WEIGHT	TIME
Challenger	30g (1oz)	90 minutes
UK First Gold	13g ($\frac{1}{2}$oz)	10 minutes from end
Protofloc	1 teaspoon	15 minutes from end
BOIL DURATION	1$\frac{1}{2}$ hours	
YEAST	Safale—DCL—S04	
TARGET FG	1041	
TARGET ABV	5%	

A WORD TO THE WISE

IPA has quite a long maturing time due to the large amount of hops that go into it.

67

PALE ALE

Pale Ale used to be brewed using a malt dried with coke. It is a great base for experimenting with different hops.

ORIGINAL GRAVITY	1049	
WATER	23 litres/5 gallons/6 US gallons	
MASH ROLL	WEIGHT	
Pale malt	3.6kg (8lb)	
Carapils	226g (8oz)	
Caramunich	226g (8oz)	
MASH SCHEDULE		
IN THE BOIL	WEIGHT	TIME
Northern Brewer	31g (1oz)	60 minutes
Fuggles	17g ($^1/_2$oz)	15 minutes from end
Goldings	11g ($^1/_4$oz)	10 minutes from end
Protofloc	1 teaspoon	15 minutes from end
BOIL DURATION	1 hour	
YEAST	British ale II—WY-1335	
TARGET FG	1013	
TARGET ABV	4.6%	

▶LIGHT SPRING ALE

Although lightly colored and refreshing, this ale is still quite heavy with a high ABV for the style.

ORIGINAL GRAVITY	1049	
WATER	23 litres/5 gallons/6 US gallons	
MASH ROLL	WEIGHT	
Pale malt	3.6kg (8lb)	
Aromatic malt	226g (8oz)	
Caravienne	226g (8oz)	
Carafa I	58g (2oz)	
MASH SCHEDULE	1$^1/_2$ hours	
IN THE BOIL	WEIGHT	TIME
Goldings	28g (1oz)	80 minutes
Goldings	14g ($^1/_2$oz)	20 minutes from end
Goldings	14g ($^1/_2$oz)	10 minutes from end
Protofloc	1 teaspoon	15 minutes from end
BOIL DURATION	1 hour 20 minutes	
YEAST	British ale II—WY-1335	
TARGET FG	1013	
TARGET ABV	4.6%	

GOLDEN SUMMER BEER

When poured into the glass, Golden Summer Beer has a hazy golden color that makes it perfect for drinking on a hot summer's day. It has a full-on, tea-and-hop aroma. Summer beer may be thin, but it is blessed with a lasting head and a delicious taste of wheat and lemon. These summery flavors are gently offset by the subtle spiciness of the coriander seeds which are added at the end of the boil.

ORIGINAL GRAVITY	1073	
WATER	23 litres/5 gallons/6 US gallons	
MASH ROLL	WEIGHT	
Maris otter	5.2kg (11½lb)	
MASH SCHEDULE	1 hour	
IN THE BOIL	WEIGHT	TIME
Hallertauer	15g (½oz)	60 minutes
Crystal	15g (½oz)	30 minutes from end
Saaz	15g (½oz)	30 minutes from end
Crystal	31g (1oz)	15 minutes from end
Coriander seeds (crushed)	1 tablespoon	30 minutes from end
Protofloc	1 teaspoon	15 minutes from end
BOIL DURATION	1 hour	
YEAST	Belgian Ardennes—WY-3522	
TARGET FG	1010	
TARGET ABV	4.5%	

BROWN ALE

Brown Ale first appeared in Northern England. The ale was commonly bought straight from the brewery. For this reason, it is sometimes known as a "running beer." With a great caramelized hue, brown ale is lighter but stronger than a mild ale.

ORIGINAL GRAVITY		
WATER	23 litres/5 gallons/6 US gallons	
MASH ROLL	WEIGHT	
Pale ale malt	2.38kg (5$\frac{1}{4}$lb)	
Caramel malt	907g (2lb)	
Chocolate malt	113g (4oz)	
MASH SCHEDULE	1 hour	
IN THE BOIL	WEIGHT	TIME
UK Fuggles	28g (1oz)	90 minutes
UK Goldings	28g (1oz)	15 minutes from end
Light brown sugar	453g (1lb)	90 minutes
BOIL DURATION	1$\frac{1}{2}$ hours	
YEAST	British ale II—WY-1335	
TARGET FG	1013	
TARGET ABV	4.32%	

OLD ALE

Traditionally, the name "old ale" was used to describe ales kept over by a brewery and sold at a premium. Sometimes, stock (or very old) ale was blended with a younger ale to tone down the acidity and create an old ale. Old ales range from 4–6.5% ABV.

ORIGINAL GRAVITY	1071	
WATER	23 litres/5 gallons/6 US gallons	
MASH ROLL	WEIGHT	
Pale ale malt	6.58kg (14$\frac{1}{2}$lb)	
Medium crystal malt	730g (1$\frac{1}{2}$lb)	
MASH SCHEDULE	1$\frac{1}{2}$ hours	
IN THE BOIL	WEIGHT	TIME
UK Fuggles	105g (3$\frac{3}{4}$oz)	90 minutes
UK Goldings	25g ($\frac{3}{4}$oz)	15 minutes from end
Protofloc	1 teaspoon	15 minutes from end
BOIL DURATION	1$\frac{1}{2}$ hours	
YEAST	London ale—WY-1028	
TARGET	FG1017	
TARGET ABV	7.2%	

A WORD TO THE WISE

In Brown Ale, the use of English ale yeast will achieve a sweeter finish. If you prefer to have a mid-range outcome, then try using a London ale yeast instead.

A WORD TO THE WISE

Mild ales are quick to drink but please bear in mind that they are also quick to go off.

 MILD

Although not highly hopped, Mild can actually be a tasty brew, especially if you enjoy malt flavors. Milds originated in 17th-century England when hops were introduced from France, Germany, and Holland. English brewers could then reduce the gravity of strong ales, using the hops for their preserving qualities, and thus produce a good all-round brew. Mild is a nice recipe for the homebrewer, although the challenge is to get big flavor into this style of brewing.

ORIGINAL GRAVITY	1032	
WATER	23 litres/5 gallons/6 US gallons	
MASH ROLL	Weight	
Pale ale malt	3.1kg ($6^3/_4$lb)	
Medium crystal malt	215g ($7^1/_2$oz)	
Chocolate malt	110g ($3^3/_4$oz)	
Torrified Wheat	100g ($3^1/_2$oz)	
MASH SCHEDULE	1 hour	
IN THE BOIL	Weight	Time
UK Challenger	18g ($^1/_2$oz)	90 minutes
UK Fuggle	10g ($^1/_4$oz)	90 minutes
UK Goldings	10g ($^1/_4$oz)	10 minutes from end
Protofloc	1 teaspoon	15 minutes from end
BOIL DURATION	$1^1/_2$ hours	
YEAST	London ale—WY-1028	
TARGET FG	1009	
TARGET ABV	3.1%	

"No soldier can fight unless he is properly fed on beef and beer."
JOHN CHURCHILL,
FIRST DUKE OF MARLBOROUGH (1650-1722)

DARK RUBY MILD

A great mild ale, Dark Ruby Mild has a sweet malty base and a slight hop balance. When you pour this ale into your glass, it should have a gorgeous, ruby-red color as well as a creamy colored, almost tan, head. This is very much an easy-drinking beer in spite of the higher ABV. Warming and delicious, it is just the tipple to imbibe sitting in front of a roaring fire on a cold winter's evening.

ORIGINAL GRAVITY	1034
WATER	23 litres/5 gallons/6 US gallons

MASH ROLL	WEIGHT	
Maris otter	5kg (11lb)	
Chocolate malt	113g (4oz)	
Medium crystal malt	1.5g ($^1/_{32}$oz)	

MASH SCHEDULE	1 hour

IN THE BOIL	WEIGHT	TIME
Williamette	41g (1$^1/_2$oz)	90 minutes
Fuggles	35g (1$^1/_4$oz)	90 minutes
UK Goldings	20g ($^3/_4$oz)	15 minutes from end
Protofloc	1 teaspoon	15 minutes from end

BOIL DURATION	1$^1/_2$ hours
YEAST	West Yorkshire Ale—WY-1469
TARGET FG	1014
TARGET ABV	5.6%

"When I read about the evils of drinking, I gave up reading."
HENNY YOUNGMAN (1906-1998)

 PORTER

First popular in the 1800s, porter (which isn't as rich as stout) is the result of using pale malts and black malt.

ORIGINAL GRAVITY	1049	
WATER	23 litres/5 gallons/6 US gallons	
MASH ROLL	WEIGHT	
Pale ale malt	4.30g (9½lb)	
Medium crystal malt	425g (15oz)	
Torrified wheat	380g (13½oz)	
Roasted barley	240g (8½oz)	
MASH SCHEDULE	1 hour	
IN THE BOIL	WEIGHT	TIME
Williamette	21g (¾oz)	90 minutes
UK Progress	8g (¼oz)	45 minutes from end
UK Fuggles	15g (½oz)	10 minutes from end
Protofloc	1 teaspoon	15 minutes from end
BOIL DURATION	1½ hours	
YEAST	Irish ale—WY-1084	
TARGET FG	1013	
TARGET ABV	4.8%	

SMOKED PORTER

A roasted bitterness is the goal here with a smoky nose: dried fruit, coffee, and chocolate all in one.

ORIGINAL GRAVITY	1056	
WATER	23 litres/5 gallons/6 US gallons	
MASH ROLL	WEIGHT	
2-row pale malt	3.1kg (6¾lb)	
Caramalt	453g (1lb)	
Smoked malt	453g (1lb)	
Carapils	340g (12oz)	
Wheat malt	226g (8oz)	
Chocolate malt	226g (8oz)	
Black malt	58g (2oz)	
MASH SCHEDULE	1 hour	
IN THE BOIL	Weight	Time
Northern Brewer	21g (¾oz)	60 minutes
Williamette	14g (½oz)	15 minutes from end
Williamette	14g (½oz)	at flame-out
Protofloc	1 teaspoon	15 minutes from end
BOIL DURATION	1 hour	
YEAST	American ale—WY-1056	
TARGET FG	1014	
TARGET ABV	5.4%	

A WORD TO THE WISE

Porters make a great base for a variety of further flavors to be introduced. You could try coffee, chocolate, fruit, and spices. A real treat for the brewing brave!

STOUT

The development of stouts and porters is closely linked. Their huge popularity meant that a wide variety of strengths became available. Breweries would often advertise these differing strengths with words like "extra" and "double." Although not universal, these words are the ones that are most commonly used when describing dark beers. Stout porters are those beers with a high gravity, usually 7–8% ABV. Irish stouts, such as Guinness, are best described as dry stouts.

ORIGINAL GRAVITY	1045	
WATER	23 litres/5 gallons/6 US gallons	
MASH ROLL	WEIGHT	
Pale ale malt	4.45kg (9³/₄lb)	
Roasted barley	465g (16¹/₂oz)	
MASH SCHEDULE	1 hour	
IN THE BOIL	WEIGHT	TIME
UK Target	25g (³/₄oz)	90 minutes
UK Goldings	12g (¹/₂oz)	10 minutes from end
Protofloc	1 teaspoon	15 minutes from end
BOIL DURATION	1¹/₂ hours	
YEAST	London ale—WY-1026	
TARGET FG	1011	
TARGET ABV	4.6%	

A WORD TO THE WISE

Try adding 70g (2¹/₂oz) of cocoa powder and 30g (1oz) of dried chili flakes at the end of the boil. If you fancy giving this a try, also add 5g (¹/₈oz) of Fuggles hops to even things out.

81

CHOCOLATE STOUT

Malt that is kilned until it has developed a chocolate flavor is used in this brew along with cocoa powder. Some brewers will use adjuncts, such as chocolate nibs, as well as flavorings, such as cranberry, blackberry, and instant coffee, or even make the beer into a double chocolate stout. However, chocolate stout can only be classified as such if chocolate has been added to the brew (and not if the chocolate flavor comes from the malt).

ORIGINAL GRAVITY	1043	
WATER	23 litres/5 gallons/6 US gallons	
MASH ROLL	WEIGHT	
Maris otter	3.6kg (8lb)	
Chocolate malt	420g (14³⁄₄oz)	
Torrified wheat	260g (9oz)	
Roasted barley	195g (6³⁄₄oz)	
Caramunich III	200g (7oz)	
MASH SCHEDULE	1 hour	
IN THE BOIL	WEIGHT	TIME
Northern Brewer	38g (1¹⁄₄oz)	90 minutes
Cocoa powder	50g (1³⁄₄oz)	15 minutes from end
Protofloc	1 teaspoon	15 minutes from end
BOIL DURATION	1¹⁄₂ hours	
YEAST	American ale—WY-1056	
TARGET FG	1011	
TARGET ABV	4%	

"The problem with the world is that everyone is a few drinks behind."
HUMPHREY BOGART (1899-1957)

84

A WORD TO THE WISE

For Coffee Stout, you will need two-thirds of a cup of dry malt extract and 3 tablespoons of dark roasted instant coffee. Bottle-condition for at least a month.

OATMEAL STOUT

Oatmeal Stout was once considered restorative and nourishing because of the oatmeal used in the mash.

ORIGINAL GRAVITY	1062	
WATER	23 litres/5 gallons/6 US gallons	

MASH ROLL	WEIGHT	
2-row malt	3.8kg (8¼lb)	
Special B	340g (12oz)	
Chocolate malt	226g (8oz)	
Carafa II	340g (12oz)	
Roasted barley	226g (8oz)	
Pale wheat malt	226g (8oz)	
Oat flakes	453g (1lb)	

MASH SCHEDULE	1½ hours	

IN THE BOIL	WEIGHT	TIME
Pacific Gem	14g (½oz)	60 minutes
Hallertauer	28g (1oz)	15 minutes from end
Hallertauer	14g (½oz)	5 minutes from end
Protofloc	1 teaspoon	15 minutes from end

BOIL DURATION	1 hour	
YEAST	Irish ale—WY-1084	
TARGET FG	1012	
TARGET ABV	6.5%	

COFFEE STOUT

Dark roasted malts are used in this stout to lend a bitter, coffee flavor alongside ground or instant coffee.

Original gravity	1086	
Water	23 litres/5 gallons/6 US gallons	

MASH ROLL	WEIGHT	
Maris otter	5.4kg (12lb)	
Torrified wheat	453g (1lb)	
Chocolate malt	226g (8oz)	
Roasted barley	226g (8oz)	
Dark crystal malt	453g (1lb)	
Coarsely ground coffee beans	226g (8oz)	

MASH SCHEDULE	1½ hours	

IN THE BOIL	WEIGHT	TIME
Northern Brewer	56g (2oz)	60 minutes
Galena	28g (1oz)	30 minutes from end
Spalt	28g (1oz)	5 minutes from end

BOIL DURATION	1 hour	
YEAST	Belgian ale—WY-1388	
TARGET FG	1018	
TARGET ABV	8.5%	

85

BARLEY WINE

Barley Wine was a seasonal beer, historically brewed at harvest time using only the freshest malts and copious amounts of Kent Goldings hops. Barley Wine made from grain rather than fruit is actually a beer!

ORIGINAL GRAVITY	1098	
WATER	23 litres/5 gallons/6 US gallons	
MASH ROLL	WEIGHT	
Maris otter malt	4.26kg (9$\frac{1}{4}$lb)	
Medium crystal malt	820g (1$\frac{3}{4}$lb)	
MASH SCHEDULE	1 hour	
IN THE BOIL	WEIGHT	TIME
Light liquid malt extract	3kg (6$\frac{1}{2}$lb)	90 minutes
Light brown sugar	580g (1$\frac{1}{4}$lb)	90 minutes
Dark brown sugar	350g (12$\frac{1}{4}$oz)	90 minutes
Northdown	46g (1$\frac{1}{2}$oz)	90 minutes
UK Goldings	15g ($\frac{1}{2}$oz)	10 minutes from end
Protofloc	1 teaspoon	15 minutes from end
BOIL DURATION	1$\frac{1}{2}$ hours	
YEAST	British ale—WY-1098	
TARGET FG	1015	
TARGET ABV	11.2%	

SCOTCH ALE

"Wee Heavy," this sweet, full-bodied ale has a low hop content and tastes of toffee and caramel. Thick and malty, Scotch Ale uses specialty malts to bring out its full character.

ORIGINAL GRAVITY	1070	
WATER	23 litres/5 gallons/6 US gallons	
MASH ROLL	WEIGHT	
Pale ale malt	3.4kg (7$\frac{1}{2}$lb)	
Amber malt	450g (1lb)	
Dark crystal malt	172g (6oz)	
Roasted barley	27g (1oz)	
MASH SCHEDULE	1 hour	
IN THE BOIL	WEIGHT	TIME
UK Goldings	28g (1oz)	90 minutes
BOIL DURATION	1$\frac{1}{2}$ hours	
YEAST	Scottish ale—WY-1728	
TARGET FG	1020	
TARGET ABV	7.5%	

A WORD TO THE WISE

Although I have used UK Goldings, throw in any old hops that you have left over as they are only needed for bittering. Use a pinch of peated malt for an added smoky flavor.

A WORD TO THE WISE

If we were to use a full-grain recipe for this Barley Wine, the total grain weight would be 8.19kg (18lb)!

CHAPTER 3

GERMAN BEERS

WEISSBIER

This beer is also sometimes known as Weizenbier. Weissbier is a Bavarian specialty beer and, according to German law, any weissbiers that are brewed in Germany must be top-fermented. This German beer is highly distinctive in that it has exotic banana and clove notes. These flavors are achieved in the beer as a by-product of fermentation and are what you are aiming for when brewing the beer. You will also be looking out for a generous head of foam.

ORIGINAL GRAVITY	1056	
WATER	23 litres/5 gallons/6 US gallons	
MASH ROLL	**WEIGHT**	
Pale wheat malt	2.4kg (5^1/$_4$lb)	
Pilsner malt	2kg (4^1/$_2$lb)	
Carapils	226g (8oz)	
Rice hulls	226g (8oz)	
MASH SCHEDULE	1 hour	
IN THE BOIL	**WEIGHT**	**TIME**
Hallertauer Hersbrucker	23g (^{3}/$_4$oz)	60 minutes
Tettnanger	14g (^{1}/$_2$oz)	15 minutes from end
Protofloc	1 teaspoon	15 minutes from end
BOIL DURATION	1 hour	
YEAST	Weihenstephan Weizen—WY-3068	
TARGET FG	1014	
TARGET ABV	5.5%	

ROGGENBIER

A specialty beer originating from Bavaria, with dominant grain flavors and a rich, creamy white head.

ORIGINAL GRAVITY	1034	
WATER	23 litres/5 gallons/6 US gallons	
MASH ROLL	WEIGHT	
2-row pale malt	3.9kg (8½lb)	
Cararye	1kg (2¼lb)	
Light crystal malt	481g (17oz)	
MASH SCHEDULE	1 hour	
IN THE BOIL	WEIGHT	TIME
Tettnanger	21g (³/₄oz)	60 minutes
Hallertauer Mittlefreuh	14g (¹/₂oz)	30 minutes from end
Saaz	12g (¹/₂oz)	30 minutes from end
Hallertauer Mittlefreuh	12g (¹/₂oz)	5 minutes from end
Saaz	14g (¹/₂oz)	5 minutes from end
Protofloc	1 teaspoon	15 minutes from end
BOIL DURATION	1 hour	
YEAST	Bavarian wheat—WY-3638	
TARGET FG	1008	
TARGET ABV	4.5%	

► RAUCHBIER

Meaning simply "smoked beer," this is an unusual beer style. Rauchbiers are incredibly hard to come by today.

ORIGINAL GRAVITY	1050	
WATER	23 litres/5 gallons/6 US gallons	
MASH ROLL	WEIGHT	
Rauch malt	3.24kg (7lb)	
Vienna malt	1.16kg (2½lb)	
Munich malt	1.16kg (2½lb)	
Chocolate malt	230g (8oz)	
MASH SCHEDULE	1 hour	
IN THE BOIL	WEIGHT	TIME
Sterling	16g (¹/₂oz)	60 minutes
Czech Saaz	28g (1oz)	15 minutes from end
Crystal	28g (1oz)	10 minutes from end
Protofloc	1 teaspoon	15 minutes from end
BOIL DURATION	1 hour	
YEAST	Bavarian lager—WY-2206	
TARGET	FG1013	
TARGET ABV	4.9%	

A WORD TO THE WISE

If you have a sweet palate, opt for a Helles Beer because it is less bitter than a Pilsner.

HELLES BEER

"Helles" means "light one" in German and this brew is indeed a light, straw-colored blonde beer. It is both sparkling and light, but do not be fooled because this really is a full-bodied brew. Light refers only to the subtle coloring and not to the alcoholic strength, which packs quite a punch. A Helles Beer should have a mild, malty flavor in the finish and should also be dry with a dilatory note of hops.

ORIGINAL GRAVITY	1048	
WATER	23 litres/5 gallons/6 US gallons	
MASH ROLL	WEIGHT	
German 2-row Pilsner malt	3.6kg (8lb)	
Munich malt	113g (4oz)	
Carafoam	340g (12oz)	
German Vienna malt	340g (12oz)	
MASH SCHEDULE	1 hour	
IN THE BOIL	WEIGHT	TIME
Hallertauer Mittelfrueh	31g (1oz)	60 minutes
Hallertauer Mittelfrueh	15g (½oz)	15 minutes from end
Czech Saaz	15g (½oz)	1 minute from end
Protofloc	1 teaspoon	15 minutes from end
BOIL DURATION	1 hour	
YEAST	Bohemian lager—WY-2124	
TARGET FG	1010	
TARGET ABV	5%	

"Not all chemicals are bad. Without chemicals such as hydrogen and oxygen, for example, there would be no way to make water, a vital ingredient in beer."
DAVE BARRY (B.1947)

93

BOCK BEER

This is a heavy, malty brew. Incredibly smooth, it is not one to knock back, but to sip, savor, and enjoy.

ORIGINAL GRAVITY	1067	
WATER	23 litres/5 gallons/6 US gallons	

MASH ROLL	WEIGHT	
German Pils malt	2.7kg (6lb)	
Dark Munich malt	1.3kg (2³/₄lb)	
Light Munich malt	1.3kg (2³/₄lb)	
Caramunich II	340g (12oz)	
Belgian special B	113g (4oz)	
German carafa special II	56g (2oz)	

MASH SCHEDULE	1 hour	

IN THE BOIL	WEIGHT	TIME
Hallertauer	14g (¹/₂oz)	90 minutes
Magnum	7g (¹/₄oz)	60 minutes from end
Hallertauer	21g (³/₄oz)	60 minutes from end
Hallertauer	14g (¹/₂oz)	10 minutes from end
Protofloc	1 teaspoon	15 minutes from end

BOIL DURATION	1¹/₂ hours
YEAST	Bohemian lager—WY-2124
TARGET FG	1015
TARGET ABV	5.5%

DOPPELBOCK

Released for the first time in 1780, "double bock" is so called because of the large quantity of grain to water.

ORIGINAL GRAVITY	1072	
WATER	23 litres/5 gallons/6 US gallons	

MASH ROLL	WEIGHT	
Pilsner malt	4.25kg (9¹/₄lb)	
Munich I	1.1kg (2¹/₂lb)	
Lager malt	662g (1¹/₂lb)	
Dark crystal malt	449g (1lb)	
Chocolate malt	90g (3oz)	

MASH SCHEDULE	1 hour	

IN THE BOIL	WEIGHT	TIME
Crystal	13g (¹/₂oz)	60 minutes
Tettnanger	28g (1oz)	60 minutes
Crystal	28g (1oz)	30 minutes from end
Protofloc	1 teaspoon	15 minutes from end

BOIL DURATION	1 hour
YEAST	Munich lager—WY-2308
TARGET FG	1018
TARGET ABV	7.2%

SCHWARZBIER

Meaning "black beer," this brew has a clean lager taste and great tones of chocolate, coffee, and vanilla.

ORIGINAL GRAVITY	1054	
WATER	23 litres/5 gallons/6 US gallons	
MASH ROLL	**WEIGHT**	
Munich malt	2kg (4^1/$_2$lb)	
Vienna malt	2kg (4^1/$_2$lb)	
Munich dark malt	453g (1lb)	
Carafa III	226g (8oz)	
Caramunich	226g (8oz)	
MASH SCHEDULE	1 hour	
IN THE BOIL	**WEIGHT**	**TIME**
Perle	28g (1oz)	65 minutes
Perle	28g (1oz)	10-day dry hop
BOIL DURATION	1 hour 5 minutes	
YEAST	Bavarian lager—WY- 2206	
TARGET FG	1014	
TARGET ABV	4.8%	

DUNKLES

Meaning simply "dark" beer, this is a full-bodied beer which has a fantastic, nutty, rounded finish.

ORIGINAL GRAVITY	1048	
WATER	23 litres/5 gallons/6 US gallons	
MASH ROLL	**WEIGHT**	
German wheat malt	1.7kg (3^3/$_4$lb)	
German 2-row Pilsner malt	1.3kg (2^3/$_4$lb)	
Vienna malt	680g (1^1/$_2$lb)	
Munich malt	453g (11b)	
Caramunich	285g (10oz)	
Chocolate malt	27g (1oz)	
MASH SCHEDULE	1 hour	
IN THE BOIL	**WEIGHT**	**TIME**
Tettnanger	40g (1^1/$_2$oz)	60 minutes
Hallertau Hersbrucker	8g (^{1}/$_4$oz)	15 minutes from end
Protofloc	1 teaspoon	15 minutes from end
BOIL DURATION	1 hour	
YEAST	Bavarian wheat—WY- 3638	
TARGET FG	1010	
TARGET ABV	5.4%	

KELLERBIER

This beer is renowned for being served before dinner as an appetite stimulant. It means "cellar beer" and is highly flavored with aromatic hops. Kellerbier has a great amber color because it contains caramalized malt. It would normally be matured unbunged in a wooden barrel, typically with very little effervescence. For this reason, not much in the way of a foamy head is formed when the beer is poured into the glass.

ORIGINAL GRAVITY	1051	
WATER	23 litres/5 gallons/6 US gallons	
MASH ROLL	WEIGHT	
German 2-row Pilsner malt	3.6kg (8lb)	
Munich malt	1.8kg (4lb)	
Chocolate malt	113g (4oz)	
MASH SCHEDULE	1 hour	
IN THE BOIL	WEIGHT	TIME
Saaz	56g (2oz)	75 minutes
Hallertauer Hersbrucker	28g (4oz)	10 minutes from end
Protofloc	1 teaspoon	15 minutes from end
BOIL DURATION	1¼ hours	
YEAST	German ale—WY-1007	
TARGET FG	1013	
TARGET ABV	5.2%	

"Give me a woman who loves beer and I will conquer the world."
KAISER WILHELM II (1859-1941)

KOLLSCH

This is the German version of a British pale ale. Traditionally brewed in Cologne, it is one of the palest German beers and one of only a handful of traditional German ales. Apparently, Kolsch is the only language that you can drink, as the word "kollsch" means "Cologne-ish," the local dialect. It is a subtle and delicate brew, making it a fantastic beer for summer quaffing.

ORIGINAL GRAVITY	1046	
WATER	23 litres/5 gallons/6 US gallons	
MASH ROLL	WEIGHT	
German wheat malt	1.1kg (2½lb)	
Munich malt	1.1kg (2½lb)	
German 2-row Pilsner malt	1kg (2¼lb)	
Vienna malt	1kg (2¼lb)	
Carapils	935g (2lb)	
MASH SCHEDULE	1 hour	
IN THE BOIL	WEIGHT	TIME
Tettnanger	28g (1oz)	60 minutes
Hallertauer	14g (½oz)	30 minutes from end
Czech Saaz	14g (½oz)	5 minutes from end
Czech Saaz	14g (½oz)	1 minute from end
Hallertauer	14g (½oz)	1 minute from end
Protofloc	1 teaspoon	15 minutes from end
BOIL DURATION	1 hour	
YEAST	Kolsch—WY- 2565	
TARGET FG	1008	
TARGET ABV	5.1%	

101

HEFEWEIZEN

This is a beer style that is usually full-bodied, fruity, and sweet. Hefeweizens are lightly hopped and made with an equal quantity of barley and wheat malts. You may notice a yeast sediment with this beer, so pour your brew with care unless you enjoy the cloudiness created by the yeast. For absolute authenticity, serve this beer in a tall, elegant glass that tapers gently down to the bottom. This is a top-fermented and bottle-conditioned beer.

ORIGINAL GRAVITY	1048	
WATER	23 litres/5 gallons/6 US gallons	
MASH ROLL	WEIGHT	
German Pilsner malt	2.5kg (5½lb)	
German wheat malt	2.5kg (5½lb)	
MASH SCHEDULE	1 hour	
IN THE BOIL	WEIGHT	TIME
Hallertauer Hersbrucker	35g (1¼oz)	60 minutes
Hallertauer Hersbrucker	7g (¼oz)	15 minutes from end
Hallertauer Hersbrucker	14g (½oz)	5 minutes from end
Protofloc	1 teaspoon	15 minutes from end
BOIL DURATION	1 hour	
YEAST	Weihenstephen Weizen—WY-3068	
TARGET FG	1008	
TARGET ABV	4.3%	

A WORD TO THE WISE

Wheat beers such as Hefeweizen were orginally banned by the German Purity Laws because they contained ingredients other than malted barley, hops and water.

OKTOBERFEST

Originating in Bavaria, this beer is an adaptation of Viennese lager with a higher alcohol level, producing a noticeable (if low) hop bitterness. Traditionally brewed in March, this beer is matured in cellar caves in readiness for the fall festivities, known as the Oktoberfest, which take place in Munich, Bavaria, in late September. This beer festival has become an important date in the German calendar since the first event was held in 1810.

ORIGINAL GRAVITY	1062	
WATER	23 litres/5 gallons/6 US gallons	
MASH ROLL	WEIGHT	
Vienna malt	3.6kg (8lb)	
Munich malt	453g (1lb)	
Caramel malt	226g (8oz)	
Pilsner malt	226g (8oz)	
MASH SCHEDULE	1 hour	
IN THE BOIL	WEIGHT	TIME
Tettnanger	28g (1oz)	60 minutes
Saaz	28g (1oz)	30 minutes from end
Protofloc	1 teaspoon	15 minutes from end
BOIL DURATION	1 hour	
YEAST	Octoberfest lager blend—WY-2633	
TARGET FG	1015	
TARGET ABV	5.7%	

CHAPTER 4

AMERICAN BEERS

PALE ALE

This is one of the world's most popular beer styles, with a high proportion of pale malts giving rise to a lighter color.

ORIGINAL GRAVITY	1045	
WATER	23 litres/5 gallons/6 US gallons	
MASH ROLL	WEIGHT	
2-row pale malt	3.8kg (8¼lb)	
Carapils	226g (8oz)	
Light crystal malt	226g (8oz)	
MASH SCHEDULE	1 hour	
IN THE BOIL	WEIGHT	TIME
Amarillo	14g (½oz)	60 minutes
Amarillo	14g (½oz)	15 minutes from end
Citra	28g (1oz)	15 minutes from end
Amarillo	28g (1oz)	1 minute from end
Citra	28g (1oz)	1 minute from end
Amarillo	28g (1oz)	14-day dry hop
Protofloc	1 teaspoon	15 minutes from end
BOIL DURATION	1 hour	
YEAST	American ale—WY-1056	
TARGET FG	1010	
TARGET ABV	4.5%	

STEAM BEER

The name for "steam beer" is perplexing since there is no definite source for it. Some say the name arose because it was made with lager yeasts at high temperatures, which made it so effervescent that it needed to let off steam! Other sources suggest it was a German variety of beer called "Dampfbier," perhaps used by American brewers of German descent. Once known for being inexpensive and of low-quality, it has now been reinvented as a craft beer.

ORIGINAL GRAVITY	1049	
WATER	23 litres/5 gallons/6 US gallons	
MASH ROLL	WEIGHT	
Pale ale malt	4.5kg (9¾lb)	
Caramel malt	136g (4¾oz)	
Carapils	123g (4¼oz)	
MASH SCHEDULE	1 hour	
IN THE BOIL	WEIGHT	TIME
Northern Brewer	38g (1¼oz)	60 minutes
Northern Brewer	13g (½oz)	15 minutes from end
Northern Brewer	17g (½oz)	5 minutes from end
Protofloc	1 teaspoon	15 minutes from end
BOIL DURATION	1 hour	
YEAST	California lager—WY-2112	
TARGET FG	1015	
TARGET ABV	4.5%	

A WORD TO THE WISE

Steam Beer has strong associations with California and sometimes goes by the name of California Common Beer.

"I am a firm believer in the people. If given the truth, they can be depended upon to meet any national crisis. The great point is to bring them the real facts, and beer."

ABRAHAM LINCOLN (1809-1865)

CREAM ALE

This is a light, crisp ale that is perfect for drinking in the summer months. Some types of cream ale have plentiful hop characters. Interestingly, cream ale was once a pre-prohibition ale in the United States, and came in two distinguishable varieties. These were Dark Common Beer and Regular Cream Common Beer. Now the ale is cold-conditioned to give its nice clean finish.

ORIGINAL GRAVITY	1057	
WATER	23 litres/5 gallons/6 US gallons	
MASH ROLL	WEIGHT	
Pilsner malt	1.5kg (3^1/4lb)	
2-row pale malt	1.5kg (3^1/4lb)	
Flaked corn	227g (8oz)	
Sugar	227g (8oz)	
MASH SCHEDULE	1^1/4 hours	
IN THE BOIL	WEIGHT	TIME
Liberty	23g (^{3}/4oz)	60 minutes
Liberty	8g (^{1}/4oz)	1 minute from end
Protofloc	1 teaspoon	15 minutes from end
BOIL DURATION	1 hour	
YEAST	American ale—WY-1056	
TARGET FG	1010	
TARGET ABV	5.4%	

111

MILK STOUT

Sweet and smooth, this brew is a great introduction to the world of heavier beers, such as traditional stouts and porters. Do not be misled by the name, however. This beer does not contain any milk. Instead, lactose (the sugar that is found in milk) is added at the end of the boiling stage. You should find that the lactose will take the edge off the bitterness that is typical of many stouts and porters, leaving you with a deliciously smooth beer.

ORIGINAL GRAVITY	1062		
WATER	23 litres/5 gallons/6 US gallons		
MASH ROLL	WEIGHT		
2-row pale malt	3kg (6$\frac{1}{2}$lb)		
Roasted barley	460g (1lb)		
Medium crystal malt	340g (12oz)		
Chocolate malt	340g (12oz)		
Munich malt	340g (12oz)		
Flaked barley	283g (10oz)		
Flaked oats	226g (8oz)		
MASH SCHEDULE	1$\frac{1}{2}$ hours		
IN THE BOIL	WEIGHT	TIME	
Magnum	10g ($\frac{1}{4}$oz)	60 minutes	
Goldings	28g (1oz)	10 minutes from end	
Protofloc	1 teaspoon	15 minutes from end	
Lactose	460g (1lb)	10 minutes from end	
BOIL DURATION	1 hour		
YEAST	Irish ale—WY-1084		
TARGET FG	1022		
TARGET ABV	5%		

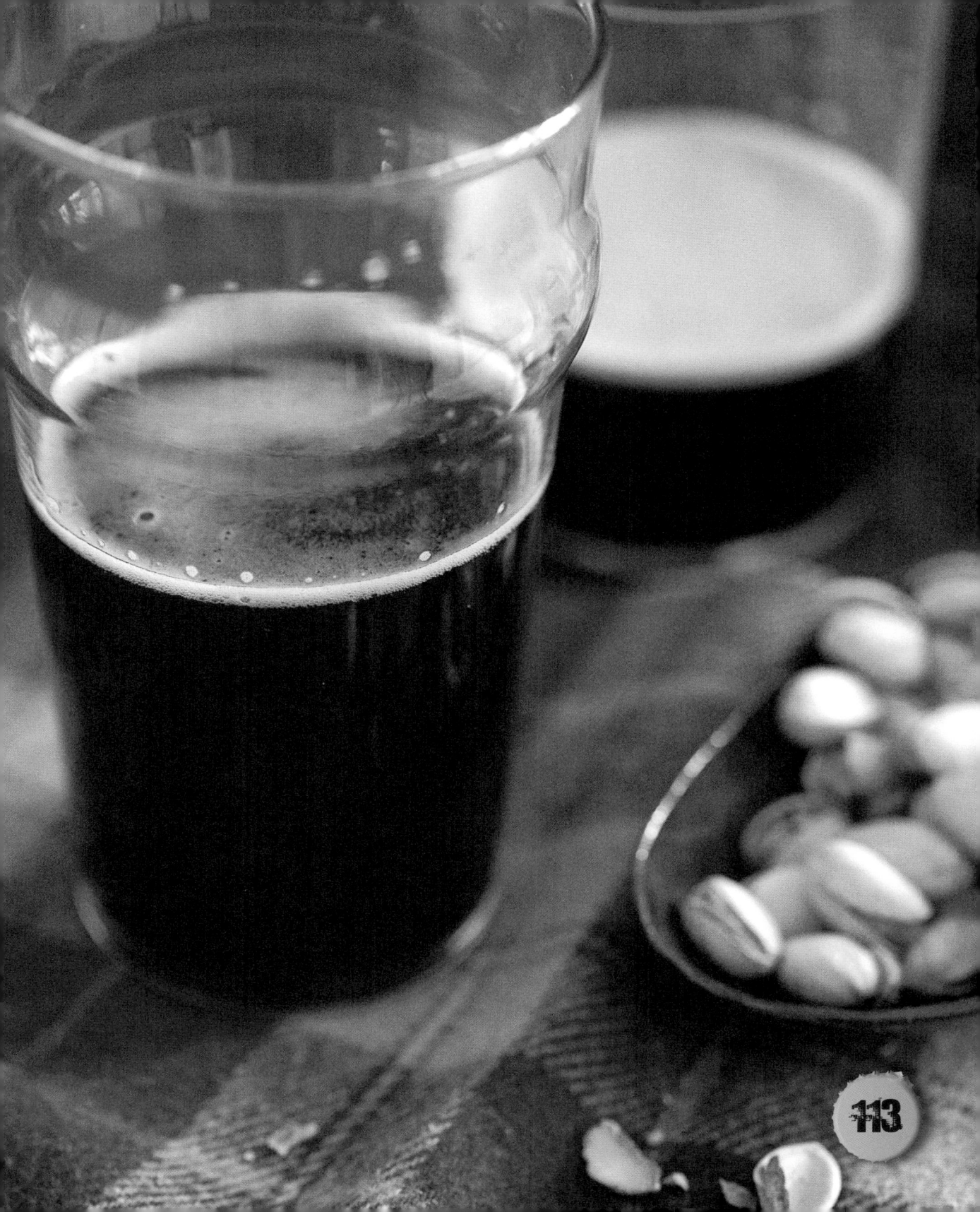

"Beer is proof that God loves us and wants us to be happy."
BENJAMIN FRANKLIN (1706–1790)

114

A WORD TO THE WISE

You can keep down the cost of brewing a pale lager by using adjuncts such as corn and rice, although some pale lagers are adjunct-free and will have a more robust level of malt and hops.

DOUBLE STOUT

Full-bodied and packed with rich flavors, American Double Stouts are strong on both alcohol and taste.

ORIGINAL GRAVITY	1123	
WATER	23 litres/5 gallons/6 US gallons	
MASH ROLL	**WEIGHT**	
Crystal malt (dark)	1.8kg (4lb)	
Chocolate malt	910g (2lb)	
Roasted wheat	453g (1lb)	
Crystal malt (dark)	453g (1lb)	
Black patent malt	226g (8oz)	
Pale chocolate malt	226g (8oz)	
Coffee malt	226g (8oz)	
MASH SCHEDULE	1½ hours	
IN THE BOIL	**WEIGHT**	**TIME**
Northern Brewer	28g (1oz)	60 minutes
Williamette	28g (1oz)	15 minutes from end
Protofloc	1 teaspoon	15 minutes from end
BOIL DURATION	1 hour	
YEAST	American ale—WY-1056	
TARGET FG	1032	
TARGET ABV	12%	

PALE LAGER

American pale lagers are made from an all-malt mash, so have a stronger malt flavor than those made with rice or corn.

ORIGINAL GRAVITY	1050	
WATER	23 litres/5 gallons/6 US gallons	
MASH ROLL	**WEIGHT**	
2-row pale malt	4kg (8¾lb)	
Dark crystal malt	311g (11oz)	
Carapils	57g (2oz)	
MASH SCHEDULE	1 hour	
IN THE BOIL	**WEIGHT**	**TIME**
Columbus	24g (¾oz)	85 minutes
Cascade	21g (¾oz)	30 minutes from end
Cascade	23g (¾oz)	5 minutes from end
Cascade	23g (¾oz)	at flame-out
Protofloc	1 teaspoon	15 minutes from end
Cascade	14g (½oz)	dry-hop after 5 days
BOIL DURATION	1 hour 25 minutes	
YEAST	American lager—WY-2035	
TARGET FG	1010	
TARGET ABV	5.5%	

AMBER ALE

American amber ales have a stronger caramel flavor and are darker in color than pale ales.

ORIGINAL GRAVITY		
WATER	23 litres/5 gallons/6 US gallons	
MASH ROLL	WEIGHT	
2-row pale malt	2.4kg (5$\frac{1}{4}$lb)	
Caramel malt	1kg (2$\frac{1}{4}$lb)	
Munich malt	910g (2lb)	
Biscuit malt	226g (8oz)	
Wheat malt	113g (4oz)	
MASH SCHEDULE	1 hour	
IN THE BOIL	WEIGHT	TIME
Amarillo	28g (1oz)	60 minutes
Centennial	14g ($\frac{1}{2}$oz)	15 minutes from end
BOIL DURATION	1 hour	
YEAST	American ale—WY-1056	
TARGET FG	1012	
TARGET ABV	7.2%	

GOLDEN ALE

As the name suggests, an American golden ale will be copper in color. It is lighter in body than typical pale ales.

ORIGINAL GRAVITY	1059	
WATER	23 litres/5 gallons/6 US gallons	
MASH ROLL	WEIGHT	
2-row malt	2.3kg (5lb)	
Pilsen malt	1.8kg (4lb)	
Munich malt	907g (2lb)	
MASH SCHEDULE	1 hour	
IN THE BOIL	WEIGHT	TIME
Cascade	14g ($\frac{1}{2}$oz)	60 minutes
Cascade	35g (1$\frac{1}{4}$oz)	30 minutes from end
Williamette	28g (1oz)	20 minutes from end
Amarillo	28g (1oz)	10 minutes from end
Williamette	7g ($\frac{1}{4}$oz)	10 minutes from end
Protofloc	1 teaspoon	15 minutes from end
BOIL DURATION	1 hour	
YEAST	American ale II—WY-1272	
TARGET FG	1015	
TARGET ABV	5.9%	

SUMMER IPA

A rich copper in color and bursting with citrusy aromas and tastes, this is a thirst-quenching summer brew.

ORIGINAL GRAVITY	1066	
WATER	23 litres/5 gallons/6 US gallons	
MASH ROLL	WEIGHT	
2-row pale malt	6kg (13$\frac{1}{4}$lb)	
Medium crystal malt	226g (8oz)	
Carapils	226g (8oz)	
MASH SCHEDULE	1 hour	
IN THE BOIL	WEIGHT	TIME
Magnum	14g ($\frac{1}{2}$oz)	60 minutes
Williamette	14g ($\frac{1}{2}$oz)	45 minutes from end
Cascade	28g (1oz)	20 minutes from end
Amarillo	28g (1oz)	10 minutes from end
Amarillo	28g (1oz)	5 minutes from end
Cascade	28g (1oz)	5 minutes from end
Amarillo	28g (1oz)	at flame-out
Protofloc	1 teaspoon	15 minutes from end
BOIL DURATION	1 hour	
YEAST	American ale—WY-1056	
TARGET FG	1012	
TARGET ABV	5%	

STRONG ALE

A potent alcohol content is one of the distinguishing characteristics of the American stong-ale style.

ORIGINAL GRAVITY	1103	
WATER	23 litres/5 gallons/6 US gallons	
MASH ROLL	WEIGHT	
2-row pale malt	8.2kg (18lb)	
Special B	566g (1$\frac{1}{4}$lb)	
Honey malt	340g (12oz)	
Wheat malt	340g (12oz)	
2-row black malt	340g (12oz)	
MASH SCHEDULE	1$\frac{1}{2}$ hours	
IN THE BOIL	WEIGHT	TIME
Chinook	28g (1oz)	60 minutes
Perle	28g (1oz)	30 minutes from end
Williamette	56g (2oz)	1 minute from end
Protofloc	1 teaspoon	15 minutes from end
BOIL DURATION	1 hour	
YEAST	American ale—WY-1056	
TARGET FG	1020	
TARGET ABV	11%	

BOURBON BEER

Beer tastes good and bourbon tastes good, so why not combine two of life's great pleasures into one delicious drink? The brewery version of this beer uses whiskey barrels to impart the flavor of the bourbon. This is a piece of equipment that's not often at the homebrewer's disposal but, luckily, French oak beans soaked in bourbon will give the brew that familiar woody flavor.

ORIGINAL GRAVITY	1071	
WATER	23 litres/5 gallons/6 US gallons	
MASH ROLL	WEIGHT	
2-row malt	2.7kg (6lb)	
Pilsen malt	2.7kg (6lb)	
Biscuit malt	226g (8oz)	
Crystal malt medium	453g (1lb)	
Honey malt	226g (8oz)	
Brown sugar	453g (1lb)	
MASH SCHEDULE	1 hour	
IN THE BOIL	Weight	Time
Centennial	9g ($^{1}/_{4}$oz)	60 minutes
Chinook	7g ($^{1}/_{4}$oz)	45 minutes from end
Amarillo	14g ($^{1}/_{2}$oz)	30 minutes from end
Liberty	28g (1oz)	15 minutes from end
Nugget	14g ($^{1}/_{2}$oz)	15 minutes from end
Cascade	14g ($^{1}/_{2}$oz)	2 minutes from end
Protofloc	1 teaspoon	15 minutes from end
Cascade	28g (1oz)	dry hop
French oak beans	56g (2oz)	14-day secondary fermenter
BOIL DURATION	1 hour	
YEAST	California lager—WY-2112	
TARGET FG	1020	
TARGET ABV	6%	

A WORD TO THE WISE

You'll need to soak the French oak beans in bourbon for 2 months before starting the recipe, adding 28g (1oz) of Colombus hops 3 weeks from the end of the soaking time.

CASCADE ALE

The name of this ale comes from Cascade, a type of hops, which provides the citrus and grapefruit flavors.

ORIGINAL GRAVITY	1045	
WATER	23 litres/5 gallons/6 US gallons	
MASH ROLL	WEIGHT	
Pilsner malt	5kg (11lb)	
Torrified wheat	226g (8oz)	
MASH SCHEDULE	1 hour	
IN THE BOIL	WEIGHT	TIME
Cascade	15g ($^{1}/_{2}$oz)	60 minutes
Saaz	15g ($^{1}/_{2}$oz)	30 minutes from end
Cascade	31g (1oz)	30 minutes from end
Saaz	15g ($^{1}/_{2}$oz)	1 minute from end
Protofloc	1 teaspoon	15 minutes from end
BOIL DURATION	1 hour	
YEAST	Belgian Ardennes—WY-3522	
TARGET FG	1010	
TARGET ABV	4%	

▶ CITRA SPECIAL

Indulge in the exotic-fruit aromas and flavors imparted by the Citra hops to this rather special beer.

ORIGINAL GRAVITY	1045	
WATER	23 litres/5 gallons/6 US gallons	
MASH ROLL	WEIGHT	
2-row pale malt	3.8kg ($8^{1}/_{4}$lb)	
Carapils	226g (8oz)	
Light crystal malt	226g (8oz)	
MASH SCHEDULE	1 hour	
IN THE BOIL	WEIGHT	Time
Citra	14g ($^{1}/_{2}$oz)	60 minutes
Citra	14g ($^{1}/_{2}$oz)	15 minutes from end
Citra	28g (1oz)	15 minutes from end
Amarillo	28g (1oz)	1 minute from end
Citra	28g (1oz)	1 minute from end
Protofloc	1 teaspoon	15 minutes from end
Citra	28g (1oz)	14-day dry hop
BOIL DURATION	1 hour	
YEAST	American ale—WY-1056	
TARGET FG	1010	
TARGET ABV	4.5%	

A WORD TO THE WISE

Use frozen strawberries and drink your Strawberry Beer young because the flavor of the fruit will be lost with age.

CHAPTER 5

FRUIT BEERS

STRAWBERRY BEER

There has been an explosion of interest in fruit-flavored beers in recent years. One of the most popular of these is Strawberry Beer. You will need to add quite a few pounds of strawberries to this fruit-driven Belgian beer, but this takes place at secondary fermentation stage. It is surprisingly light given its strength. Your beer should have a distinctive strawberry aroma, a rose-pink hue, and a head that disappears when poured.

ORIGINAL GRAVITY	1048	
WATER	23 litres/5 gallons/6 US gallons	
MASH ROLL	WEIGHT	
Torrified wheat	2.48kg (5½lb)	
Pilsner malt	2.48kg (5½lb)	
MASH SCHEDULE	1 hour	
IN THE BOIL	WEIGHT	TIME
Fuggles	31g (1oz)	90 minutes
Protofloc	1 teaspoon	15 minutes from end
Frozen strawberries (thawed)	4.53kg (10lb)	in the secondary fermentation
BOIL DURATION	1½ hours	
YEAST	Belgian wheat—WY-3942	
EXPECTED FG	1013	
EXPECTED ABV	4.8%	

RASPBERRY BEER

You're looking for a fruity aroma without disturbing the beer balance in taste and a ruby-red hue.

ORIGINAL GRAVITY	1055	
WATER	23 litres/5 gallons/6 US gallons	
MASH ROLL	WEIGHT	
Pilsner malt	2.49kg (5$\frac{1}{2}$lb)	
Wheat malt	2.49kg (5$\frac{1}{2}$lb)	
Flaked oats	226g (8oz)	
MASH SCHEDULE	1 hour	
IN THE BOIL	WEIGHT	TIME
Hallertau	28g (1oz)	60 minutes
Protofloc	1 teaspoon	15 minutes from end
Frozen raspberries (thawed)	1.13kg (2$\frac{1}{2}$lb)	in the secondary fermentation
BOIL DURATION	1 hour	
YEAST	American ale—WY-1056	
TARGET FG	1005	
TARGET ABV	4%	

PASSION FRUIT BEER

This is fruity and tropical in aroma and dangerously drinkable, with a smooth mouth-feel.

ORIGINAL GRAVITY	1048	
WATER	23 litres/5 Gallons/6 US Gallons	
MASH ROLL	WEIGHT	
Wheat malt	2kg (4$\frac{1}{2}$lb)	
2-row malt	1.6kg (3$\frac{1}{2}$lb)	
Unmalted wheat	450g (1lb)	
Munich malt	225g (8oz)	
Rice hulls	225g (8oz)	
MASH SCHEDULE	1 hour	
IN THE BOIL	WEIGHT	TIME
Hallertauer	14g ($\frac{1}{2}$oz)	60 minutes
Mt. Hood	14g ($\frac{1}{2}$oz)	40 minutes from end
Amarillo	14g ($\frac{1}{2}$oz)	5 minutes from end
Passion fruit purée	475ml (16$\frac{1}{2}$fl.oz)	5 minutes from end
Mango purée	950ml (33$\frac{1}{2}$fl.oz)	5 minutes from end
Protofloc	1 teaspoon	15 minutes from end
BOIL DURATION	1 hour	
YEAST	American ale—WY-1056	
TARGET FG	1008	
TARGET ABV	3.6%	

◄ CHERRY BEER

Use normal morello cherries as the traditional Belgian cherry called the "krieken" is difficult to find.

ORIGINAL GRAVITY	1062	
WATER	23 litres/5 gallons/6 US gallons	
MASH ROLL	WEIGHT	
Lager malt	2.3kg (5lb)	
Wheat malt	2.2kg (4¾lb)	
MASH SCHEDULE	1 hour	
IN THE BOIL	WEIGHT	TIME
Northern Brewer	22g (¾oz)	90 minutes
Morello cherries	4kg (8¾lb)	at the end
Protofloc	1 teaspoon	15 minutes from end
Pectolase	20g (¾oz)	in the fermenter
BOIL DURATION	1½ hours	
YEAST	Belgian strong ale—WY-1388	
TARGET FG	1015	
TARGET ABV	6.3%	

FIG BEER

Rich and complex in flavor, figs are less tart than berries. Vary the brew with dates, raisins, and a little vanilla.

ORIGINAL GRAVITY	1062	
WATER	23 litres/5 gallons/6 US gallons	
MASH ROLL	WEIGHT	
Pale malt	4.5kg (9¾lb)	
Carapils	113g (4oz)	
MASH SCHEDULE	1½ hours	
IN THE BOIL	WEIGHT	TIME
Amarillo	15g (½oz)	60 minutes
Protofloc	1 teaspoon	15 minutes from end
Fig purée	3.15kg (6¾lb)	in the secondary fermentor for 7 days
BOIL DURATION	1 hour	
YEAST	Irish ale—WY-1084	
TARGET FG	1010	
TARGET ABV	5.5%	

PEACH BEER

Using real fruit rather than fruit syrup is a taste revelation. Try adding grated ginger to the secondary fermenter.

ORIGINAL GRAVITY	1065	
WATER	23 litres/5 gallons/6 US gallons	

MASH ROLL	Weight	
Pale ale malt	2.72kg (6lb)	
Wheat malt	2.72kg (6lb)	
Cara amber	453g (1lb)	
Chocolate malt	113g (4oz)	

MASH SCHEDULE	1 hour	

IN THE BOIL	WEIGHT	TIME
Chinook	14g ($^1/_2$oz)	60 minutes
Chinook	14g ($^1/_2$oz)	45 minutes from end
Amarillo	14g ($^1/_2$oz)	30 minutes from end
Cascade	14g ($^1/_2$oz)	15 minutes from end
Mt.Hood	14g ($^1/_2$oz)	at the end
Frozen peaches (thawed)	1.8kg (4lb)	add to secondary fermentation
Protofloc	1 teaspoon	15 minutes from end
Amarillo	28g (1oz)	dry hop for 7 days

BOIL DURATION	1 hour	
YEAST	American ale—WY-1056	
TARGET FG	1011	
TARGET ABV	7.5%	

BLACKBERRY STOUT

A rich stout, slightly nutty, with blackberry and coffee aromas. Reaches its prime within 4-6 weeks.

ORIGINAL GRAVITY	1045	
WATER	23 litres/5 gallons/6 US gallons	

MASH ROLL	WEIGHT	
Pale ale malt	4.45kg (9$^3/_4$lb)	
Roasted barley	465g (16$^1/_2$oz)	

MASH SCHEDULE	1 hour	

IN THE BOIL	WEIGHT	TIME
UK Target	25g ($^3/_4$oz)	90 minutes
UK Goldings	12g ($^1/_2$oz)	10 minutes from end
Protofloc	1 teaspoon	15 minutes from end
Frozen blackberries (thawed)	1.18kg (2$^1/_2$lb)	add to secondary fermentation

BOIL DURATION	1$^1/_2$ hours	
YEAST	London ale—WY-1026	
TARGET FG	1011	
TARGET ABV	5.3%	

CHAPTER 6

REST OF THE WORLD BEERS

PILSNER

The Bohemian Pilsner originates from the Czech Republic. First brewed in 1842 in the city of Pilsen, from where it takes its name, Pilsner was then swiftly adapted by German brewers in order to create their own style of beer. This particular Pilsner should be pale gold in color. It should have a strong bitterness on drinking, as well as a clearly noticeable hop presence. As you drink, savor the dryness of the finish.

ORIGINAL GRAVITY	1045	
WATER	23 litres/5 gallons/6 US gallons	
MASH ROLL Pilsner malt	WEIGHT 4.75kg (10$\frac{1}{2}$lb)	
MASH SCHEDULE	1$\frac{1}{2}$ hours	
IN THE BOIL Hallertauer Tettnanger Protofloc	WEIGHT 23g ($\frac{3}{4}$oz) 20g ($\frac{3}{4}$oz) 1 teaspoon	TIME 90 minutes 10 minutes from end 15 minutes from end
BOIL DURATION	1$\frac{1}{2}$ hours	
YEAST	Czech Pilsner—WY-2278	
EXPECTED FG	1011	
EXPECTED ABV	4.5%	

VIENNESE LAGER

Originally developed in Vienna in 1841, this lager should be amber to copper in color and have a lightly bittered hop balance. The presence of Vienna and Munich malts make this lager darker than other lager styles. You may find this lager sold under a different name, Amber Lager, which is just the global interpretation of the Viennese Lager and allows for variation to the malt and hopping ratios.

ORIGINAL GRAVITY	1049	
WATER	23 litres/5 gallons/6 US gallons	
MASH ROLL	WEIGHT	
Vienna malt	4.7kg (10$^{1}/_{2}$lb)	
Munich malt	580g (1$^{1}/_{4}$lb)	
Black malt	50g (1$^{3}/_{4}$oz)	
MASH SCHEDULE	1$^{1}/_{2}$ hours	
IN THE BOIL	WEIGHT	TIME
Tettnanger	40g (1$^{1}/_{2}$oz)	90 minutes
Saaz	10g ($^{1}/_{4}$oz)	30 minutes from end
Protofloc	1 teaspoon	15 minutes from end
BOIL DURATION	1$^{1}/_{2}$ hours	
YEAST	Munich Lager—WY-2308	
TARGET FG	1012	
TARGET ABV	5%	

NEW ZEALAND JADE ALE

This is a rich and medium-bodied ale. You should find that the color will be red to brown in varying degrees. The recipe is fairly heavy on the hops like the Imperial Red Ale. This brew should develop a great malty backbone with an equally good hop aroma. If you find that it is just not hoppy enough for your taste, then try adding another 14g (half an ounce) of Pacific Jade hops 5 minutes from the end.

ORIGINAL GRAVITY	1050	
WATER	23 litres/5 gallons/6 US gallons	
MASH ROLL	WEIGHT	
Pale malt	2.5kg (5½lb)	
Munich malt	900g (2lb)	
Biscuit malt	226g (8oz)	
Wheat malt	113g (4oz)	
MASH SCHEDULE	1½ hours	
IN THE BOIL	WEIGHT	TIME
Pacific Jade	28g (1oz)	60 minutes
Pacific Jade	14g (½oz)	15 minutes from end
Protofloc	1 teaspoon	15 minutes from end
BOIL DURATION	1 hour	
YEAST	American ale—WY-1056	
TARGET FG	1012	
TARGET ABV	5%	

"Alcohol is necessary for a man so that he can have a good opinion of himself, undisturbed by the facts."
ANONYMOUS

BOKKØL

This strong lager is dark in color and also blessed with a powerful caramel characteristic on tasting. This makes it an excellent choice for serving with sweet dishes or desserts at the end of a meal, perhaps as an alternative to drinking port or madeira. Traditionally, this lager was brewed in the fall and then stored in barrels ready for drinking the following spring. It will have a gentle head when poured. You should find that it's as much of a delight to look at as it's a pleasure to drink.

ORIGINAL GRAVITY	1062	
WATER	23 litres/5 gallons/6 US gallons	

MASH ROLL	WEIGHT	
Pilsen malt	2.7kg (6lb)	
Light Munich malt	1.4kg (3lb)	
Carapils	226g (8oz)	
Light crystal malt	453g (1lb)	

MASH SCHEDULE	1½ hours

IN THE BOIL	WEIGHT	TIME
Perle	30g (1oz)	60 minutes
Tettnanger	28g (1oz)	20 minutes from end
Hallertauer	28g (1oz)	15 minutes from end
Caraway seeds (crushed)	1 teaspoon	15 minutes from end
Protofloc	1 teaspoon	15 minutes from end

BOIL DURATION	1 hour
YEAST	Bohemian lager—WY-2124
TARGET FG	1011
TARGET ABV	7%

GLOSSARY

Adjunct Any non-enzymatic fermentable. Adjuncts include unmalted cereals, such as flaked barley or corn grits, syrups, and sugars.

Aldehyde A chemical precursor to alcohol. In some cases, alcohol can be oxidized to aldehydes, creating off-flavors.

Ale A beer brewed from a top-fermenting yeast with a relatively short, warm fermentation.

Alpha Acid Units (AAU) A home-brewing measurement of hops that quantifies the amount of alpha acids (bittering agents) going into the beer before fermentation. Equal to the weight of hops in ounces multiplied by the percentage of Alpha Acids.

Amylase An enzyme group that converts starches to sugars, consisting primarily of alpha and beta amylase. Also referred to as the diastatic enzymes.

Aroma hops Hops usually added in the last 5 minutes of the boil to impart a hop aroma. They do not contribute much bitterness.

Attenuation The degree of conversion of sugar to alcohol and carbon dioxide.

Base malt A malt such as pale malt that serves as the "backbone" of the beer, as well as the main sugar source for fermentation.

Beer Any beverage made by fermenting malted barley and seasoning with hops.

Bittering hops Hops used early in he boil to impart bitterness. They do not generally impart much flavor or aroma.

Bottle conditioning Carbonating beer with an additional fermentation in the bottle.

Brew-kettle The vessel in which the wort from the mash is boiled with hops. Also called a copper.

Brewer's yeast A yeast used or suitable for use in brewing; the dried pulverized cells of such a yeast (*Saccharomyces cerevisiae*) are used especially as a source of B-complex vitamins.

"Bright" beer Beer in which yeast is no longer in suspension.

Burton water Hard water from Burton-on-Trent, in England, which is a superior water for brewing. (You can use gypsum salts to create the same hardness.)

Carboy Large glass jar specifically designed to hold wort for fermenting and for aging beer. Carboys typically range in size from 13.6–27.25 liters (3–6 gallons/3½ –7¼ US gallons). They are superior to most types of plastic fermentation and aging vessels because they do not capture or transfer odors or flavors.

Copper Another name for the boiler. Copper finings, although they are not made from copper, are meant for use in the boiler.

Demijohn A glass fermentation vessel.

Diacetyl Fermentation by-product that may lend buttery or butterscotch notes to beer. This is considered an off-flavor in excessive amounts in any beer. Note that it is considered an off-flavor in most lagers in any amount. Can also be caused by contamination.

Diastatic The conversion of starches into sugars.

Dry hopping Adding hops to finished beer to provide hop aroma and flavor but no bitterness.

Esters Aromatic compounds formed from alcohols by yeast action. Typically, smell fruity.

Fermentation The conversion of wort to beer, a process by which yeast turns sugars into alcohol and carbon dioxide.

Fermenter The vessel in which fermentation takes place; typically, a glass carboy or food-grade plastic bucket for homebrewing applications.

Final gravity (FG) The finished beer gravity will range from 1.005–1.015, depending on the original gravity (OG) and type of yeast. The density of the wort after fermentation occurs.

Finings Use of Irish moss or isinglass (or other agents) to clarify beer.

Flavor hops Hops added to the boil within the last 20 minutes, imparting flavor and some aroma to the beer and the settling of the yeast out of solution.

Flocculation Used to measure the rate at which yeast settles to the bottom of the fermentation vessel.

Gelatin A colorless and tasteless protein used as a fining agent.

Grain bill A list of the types and quantities of malt and other grains used in a beer recipe.

Gravity Like density, gravity describes the concentration of malt sugar in the wort. The specific gravity of water is 1.000 at 15°C (59°F). Typical beer worts range from 1.035–1.055 before fermentation (OG). The finished beer gravity (FG) will range from 1.005–1.015, depending on the OG and type of yeast.

Grist The term for crushed malt before mashing.

Gypsous water *See* Burton water.

Gypsum salts Hydrated calcium sulphate used to treat soft or neutral water in order to make it hard.

Homebrew Used to describe an alcoholic drink, especially beer, brewed at home. Hence, homebrewer and homebrewing.

Hop strainer A device to help strain hops to improve clarification of beer.

Hydrometer Instrument that measures the density of liquid in comparison with the density of water. You can determine the alcohol percentage of a finished beer by comparing the original gravity and final gravity.

Insulated mash tun The double-jacketed, stainless-steel vessel in which mashing occurs.

International Bittering Units (IBU) A more precise unit for measuring hops. Equal to the AAU, multiplied by factors for percent utilization, wort volume and wort gravity.

Irish moss An emulsifying agent that promotes break-material formation and precipitation during the boil and upon cooling.

Isinglass The clear swim bladders of a species of small fish, consisting mainly of the structural protein collagen, which acts to absorb and precipitate yeast cells, via electrostatic binding.

Krausen Refers to the foamy head that builds on top of the beer during primary fermentation.

Lauter To strain or separate. Lautering separates the wort from the grain via filtering and sparging.

Lovibond Measurement against which malt and beer colors are compared. The higher the lovibond, the darker the color.

Malt Any grain (rye, wheat, barley, etc.) that has undergone the malting process.

Malt liquor A legal term used in the United States to designate a fermented beverage of relatively high alcohol content (7–8% by volume).

Mash Step-in, all-grain or partial mash brewing in which crushed grains/malt are mixed with hot water to rest at a pre-determined temperature.

Mash roll List of grain needed for a specific recipe.

Mash tun A tank where grist is soaked in water and heated in order to convert the starch to sugar and extract the sugars and other solubles from the grist.

Microbrewery Breweries and brewpubs producing less than 1,500 barrels per year.

Mini-pin A small barrel that holds 5 litres (1 gallon/1¼ US gallons) of liquid.

Original gravity The density of the wort before fermentation occurs.

Petillance Means slightly fizzy to tickle the tongue.

Pitch Term for adding the yeast to the fermenter.

Poly-pin A vessel that can hold 20.5 litres (4½ gallons/5 ½ US gallons).

Primary fermentation The high-activity phase marked by the evolution of carbon dioxide and krausen. Most of the attenuation occurs during this phase.

Priming The method of adding a small amount of fermentable sugar prior to bottling to give the beer carbonation.

Protofloc A type of copper fining available in tablet form. Add it toward the end of the boil to help remove protein from the wort, which could cause hazes in the finished beer.

Racking The careful siphoning of the beer away from the trub.

Runnings The liquid collected from the mash.

Secondary fermentation A period of settling and conditioning of the beer after primary fermentation and before bottling.

"Smack-pack" yeast A form of liquid yeast. Consists of a pouch of yeast with a smaller pouch of starter wort inside. Once "smacked," the inner pouch ruptures and the yeast will begin growing. The pouch will expand to about 5cm (2in) and will be ready to pitch within a couple of days.

Sodium ion A mineral that contributes to the perceived flavor of beer by enhancing its sweetness.

Sparge To sprinkle; to rinse the grain bed during lautering.

Strike water This is water that has been heated to the right temperature to add to the grist.

Tej A mead or honey wine that is brewed and consumed in Ethiopia. It is flavored with the powdered leaves and twigs of gesho (*Rhamnus prinoides*), a hop-like bittering agent that is a species of buckthorn.

Trub The sediment at the bottom of the fermenter, consisting of hops, hot and cold break material, and dormant (sometimes dead) yeast.

Wort The malt-sugar solution that is boiled with hops prior to fermentation.

Zymurgy The science of brewing and fermentation.

Useful Abbreviations

AA	apparent attenuation
ABV	alcohol by volume
ASBC	American Society of Brewing Chemists
CO_2	carbon dioxide
CRS	Carbonate Reducing Solution
DLS	Dry Liquor Salts
DME	Dry Malt Extract
EBC	European Brewery Convention
FG	Final Gravity
IBU	International Bittering Units
°L	Lovibond
OG	Original Gravity
SRM	Standard Reference Method

EQUIPMENT SUPPLIERS

NORTH AMERICA

American Home Brew Supply
9295 Chesapeake Dr, Ste E
San Diego
California 92123
(858) 268-3024
www.redkart.com/ahbs

Beer Necessities
9850 Nesbit Ferry Road
Alpharetta
Georgia 30022
(770) 645-1777
www.beernecessities.com

Brew Brothers
2020 NW Aloclek Drive
Suite 104
Hillsboro
Oregon 97124
(971) 222 3434
www.brewbrothers.biz

Brooklyn Homebrew
163 8th Street
Brooklyn
New York 11215
(718) 369 0776
www.brooklyn-
homebrew.com

**Canadian Homebrew
Supplies**
10 Wilkinson Rd, Unit 1
Brampton
Ontario L6T 5B1
(905) 450-0191
www.homebrew-supplies.ca

Homebrew Headquarters
300 N. Colt Road, Suite 134
Richardson
Texas 75080
(972) 234-4411
www.homebrewhq.com

Home Sweet Homebrew
2008 Sansom Street
Philadelphia
PA 19103
(215) 569 9469
www.homesweethomebrew.
com

Keystone Homebrew Supply
435 Doylestown Road (Rt. 202)
Montgomeryville
PA 18936
(215) 855-0100
www.keystonehomebrew.com

**Listermann's Brewing
Supplies**
1621 Dana Avenue
Cincinnati
Ohio 45207
(513) 731-1130
www.listermann.com

**Midwest Homebrewing
and Winemaking Supplies**
5825 Excelsior Blvd.
Minneapolis
MN 55416
(952) 925-9854
www.midwestsupplies.com

**Northern Brewer
Homebrew Supply**
1150 Grand Avenue
St. Paul
Minnesota 55105
651-223-6114
www.northernbrewer.com

Riverside Wine and Spirits
600 Manufacturers Rd
Chattanooga
Tennessee 37405-3702
(423) 267-4305
www.riversidewine.com

**Rocky Mountain
Homebrew Supply**
218 N 4000 E
Rigby
Idaho 83442
(208) 745 0866
www.rockymountainhome
brew.com

**Southern Brewing
& Winemaking**
1717 East Busch Blvd.
Unit 805
Tampa
Florida 33612
(813) 374-2174
www.southernbrewingwine
making.com

UK

Brew
Unit 11
Portway Business Centre
Salisbury
SP4 6QX
0844 7362672
www.brewuk.co.uk

The Brew Shop
48 Buxton Road
Heaviley
Stockport
SK2 6NB
0161 480 4880
www.thebrewshop.com

The Brewer's Tap
70 St James Way
Sidcup
Kent
DA14 5HF
0208 302 8202
www.brewerstap.co.uk

Brewstore
14 Elgin Terrace
Edinburgh
EH7 5NW
0131 466 6244
www.brewstore.co.uk

Burghley Homebrew
Calamity Gulch
Bridge Hill Road
Newborough
Cambridgeshire
PE6 7SA
01733 810259
www.burghley-
homebrew.com

Easy Home Brew
Unit 19
Connect 10
Foster Road
Sevington
Ashford
Kent
TN24 0FE
01233 502269
www.easyhomebrew.co.uk

The Home Brew Centre
250 Freeman Street
Grimsby
DN32 9DR
01472 343435
www.homebrewcentregy.com

The Homebrew Shop
Unit 2
Blackwater Trading Estate
Blackwater Way
Aldershot
Hants
GU12 4DJ
01252 338045
www.the-home-brew-
shop.co.uk

The Hop Shop
22 Dale Road
Mutley
Plymouth
Devon
PL4 6PE
01752 660382
www.hopshopuk.com

Love Brewing
591 West Derby Road
Liverpool
L13 8AE
www.lovebrewing.co.uk

**The Online
Homebrew Company**
Unit 5 Parkside
Potters Way
Southend-on-Sea
Essex
SS2 5SJ
http://www.the-online-
homebrew-company.co.uk

Things to Brew
Unit 2
Kershaws Garden Centre
Halifax Road
Brighouse
West Yorkshire
HD6 2QD
01484 401423
www.thingstobrew.co.uk

INDEX

ACKNOWLEDGMENTS

Both Dave and I would like to extend our thanks to our friends and families for being so supportive throughout the writing of this book, when we were holed up with nothing but beer and brewing on the agenda. We are especially thankful for the patient encouragement we received from our respective partners, Elli and Chris, and also from our children, who at times must have wondered if we would ever return from the world of brewing. So Florence, Charlie, Isabel, Oscar, Silas, Rose, and Arturo, thanks for being wonderful kids!

Thank you, too, to Pete Jorgensen for his patience throughout the project, Caroline West for her keen eye for detail, and Ashley Western for the great design.

We would also like to thank Gavin Kingcome and Luis Peral-Aranda for their hard work in making the whole book look fantastic.

And last but not least, another big thank you to my husband, Chris, who is always there.

Please visit www.beshlie.co.uk to read my latest blog entries.

Beshlie Grimes

Chart on p19 from Wikipedia, "Beer Measurement" http://en.wikipedia/wiki/Beer_measurement (as of November 6th, 2011, 19:11 GMT).

9-12-13

HAT

Please renew or return items by the date
shown on your receipt

www.hertsdirect.org/libraries

Renewals and   0300 123 4049
enquiries:

Textphone for hearing   0300 123 4041
or speech impaired

Hertfordshire

CREATIVE display

CREATIVE display

INSPIRING IDEAS TO MAKE EVERY SURFACE BEAUTIFUL

GERALDINE JAMES

CICO BOOKS
LONDON NEW YORK

PUBLISHED IN 2012 BY CICO BOOKS

an imprint of Ryland Peters & Small
519 Broadway, 5th Floor, New York
NY 10012
20-21 Jockey's Fields, London
WC1R 4BW

www.cicobooks.com

10 9 8 7 6 5 4 3 2 1

PROJECT EDITOR: Gillian Haslam
CONTRIBUTING EDITOR: Helen Ridge
DESIGN: Paul Tilby
PHOTOGRAPHY: Andrew Wood
(Photographs on page 102-103,
160, 164-165, and 211 by Rick
Haylor. Photograph on page 5
courtesy of Caleb Kimbrough at
lost and taken.com)

A CIP catalog record for this book is available
from the Library of Congress and the British
Library.

ISBN: 978 1 908170 16 3

Printed in China

For digital editions, visit
www.cicobooks.com/apps.php

CONTENTS

INTRODUCTION

To me and those in my world, displaying our treasures or collections comes naturally. ALL OF US HAVE THINGS WE LOVE THAT WE WANT TO DISPLAY FOR OUR ENJOYMENT AND FOR THAT OF OTHERS. WE ALSO HAVE STORIES TO TELL ABOUT THEM AND WANT TO EXPLAIN OUR CHOICES. This is what defines us.

We seek to be individual in our homes, not wishing to follow the pack, and our displays unashamedly show off our favorite things. In the pages that follow, you will see homes from LA to Paris, but there is a common link between them: they all belong to people who inhabit creative worlds, and have the ability and confidence to put things together in ways that suit them and their lifestyles.

The rather grand lady in the portrait is the focal point of this well-balanced table display. An ornate antique mirror to the right complements it well, while a selection of vintage decorative items gives the collection additional charm.

◄◄ Taking center stage on a timeworn chest of drawers is an ornate glass dome. The tall foxed mirror reflects it all, giving the beautifully balanced display even greater impact.

►► A shelf has been specially built behind this long sofa to house a carefully curated display. The large antique clock, no longer in working order, is the central focus, while the other items create a balance of color and shape.

◄◄ In a child's bedroom, historic school photographs are displayed, one above the other, all framed by curtains that drape elegantly to the floor. A vintage child's scooter is kept next to the battered table, on which stands a desk lamp and a globe. All the pieces here are meaningful to the child, as well as being visually appealing.

◄ Postcards, pots, cups, and photographs share the personal space of this keepsake cabinet. The different elements are all pulled together very cleverly by the color blue, which gives the display a strong sense of identity and adds to its fascination.

▷ The beauty of imperfection can be clearly seen in the walls of this Parisian chateau. A simple table holds a display of favorite shoes from Christine Innamorato.

▷ ▷ The distressed walls create a setting of faded grandeur for taking afternoon tea. Arranged on a round table, washed in the palest green, is an exquisite deep turquoise tea service with a gold trim, and a plate of delicious macaroons.

The color blue makes a bold statement in this keepsake cabinet

There is so much enjoyment to be had living with your treasures or collections. In my previous book, CREATIVE WALLS, I asked you to trust your instincts and "go for it." This remains true in every sense here. IF YOU LOVE SOMETHING ENOUGH, SHOW THE WORLD HOW MUCH BY DISPLAYING IT FOR ALL TO SEE. I AM CERTAINLY NOT TELLING YOU WHAT YOU SHOULD HAVE IN YOUR DISPLAYS, MERELY TRYING TO GUIDE YOU THROUGH SOME IDEAS TO MAKE THEM WORK THE BEST THEY CAN.

There isn't a great deal of minimalism in this book, but you will see ideas that are pared down yet still CREATE A VISUAL IMPACT BECAUSE OF THE CARE TAKEN CHOOSING COLORS AND MATERIALS, and the overall balance that is achieved. Some of the displays are from the homes of the experts, people who, in their line of work, help others make design choices. Others have been created by friends who simply enjoy treating every day with a sense of occasion.

◄◄ ◄◄ All the
disparate items on
this unusual table
are precious and very
special to the owner
in one way or another.
Leaning against the
mirror is a typically
romantic painting by
Laurence Amélie; the
bird on a twig was
painted by the owner's
grandson. The vintage
items have all been
collected and chosen
for their colors, which
are perfectly balanced.

This is another well-
thought-out display of
objects collected over
time, where all the
colors complement
each other perfectly.
The nature theme is
very much in keeping
with the country-house
environment.

◄◄ An eclectic mix of engaging items shares space with hundreds of books and magazines. Combined with the imposing bust on its plinth and the vase of poppies, they make a vital and unique space.

▷► Squeezed in between two well-worn leather armchairs, a round table with unusual antler legs is piled high with books. The footstool and multicolored rug are the finishing touches to this very special environment for relaxing and reading.

▷► ▷► The bunch of wildflowers picked from the garden is the focus of this vignette. Books have been used to give height to the lamp and also form a display in their own right on the ornate metal chair.

Rich colors and a very distinctive style are on show in these rooms from across the globe

You may say this is all very well but how can I translate these ideas into my simple home? The answer is to START LOOKING AT THINGS IN A DIFFERENT WAY AND EXPERIMENT. MOVE OBJECTS AROUND IN YOUR HOME UNTIL YOU START TO SEE SHAPES EMERGING, and think about how your treasures can be shown off instead of being tucked away in a cupboard. Give your books a decorative role, for example, perhaps picking out all those in a certain color to get a theme going, or use them as the plinth for an antique candlestick, a child's naive sculpture, or a vase of flowers. See new uses for things that have had a previous life: a favorite vinyl record, no longer played, can be reincarnated as a cakestand, an old door as a coffee table. Such inventiveness will immediately give your home a rare quality.

I hope you will enjoy looking through this book as much as I have enjoyed putting it together. I would like you to use it as I intended~as a source of inspiration and a trigger for your own ideas. RECOGNIZE BEAUTY IN IMPERFECTION AND APPRECIATE UNUSUAL, OR EVEN UNIQUE, QUALITIES IN RUN-OF-THE-MILL OBJECTS. HAVE FUN AND CELEBRATE THE EVERYDAY!

DISPLAY

I live in a world where the idea of DISPLAYING ONE'S PRECIOUS BELONGINGS FOR ALL TO SEE IS QUITE NORMAL, and we use every available surface to do so. A bedside table is much more than a home for a book and a lamp. It can be used to arrange a collection of beautiful objects in a creative or stylish way, PERHAPS ADDING TO THE ROMANCE OF A ROOM OR TELLING A STORY.

Drawing inspiration from other people's lives is an addictive pastime. When you move through these pages, you may not like everything you see but YOUR MIND WILL CERTAINLY BE OPENED TO NEW IDEAS SO THAT YOU ARE INSPIRED TO LOOK DIFFERENTLY AT THE OBJECTS AROUND YOU. There are many display styles to choose from, some that entertain, some that puzzle, but there will be at least one, without question, that will suit you.

◄ ❆ ❆ ► Wooden paneling forms the backdrop in this Hollywood home. In the living room, left, a beautiful French antique mirror is the focus of the display, assisted by books and giant candlesticks. In the hallway, right, an unusual fringed standard lamp is poised to throw light onto an intimate display that includes a precious photograph of the owner's grandmother.

Books used as display serve many purposes. To start with, they look good, bringing color to a space. They can also work as a shelf or support to an ornament, and they can even be read! In these images, you can see clearly how books can become a plinth to accentuate another object and give it extra height, or how CAREFULLY CHOSEN BOOKS IN SHADES OF THE SAME COLOR AND PLACED IN JUST THE RIGHT WAY, CREATE FORM AND A STRIKING VISION.

The books themselves may be unearthed at secondhand bookshops or antiques markets. They may be favorite stories from childhood, or the complete works of a certain poet or playwright. On the other hand, their subject matter may be of little importance and you could cover them in fabrics or paper to enhance or unify the color palette of a surface or room.

← A Paisley cloth covers the top of a console table, where a coordinated display of books and crystals has been created.

This mystical and intriguing display is made up of a collection of natural curiosities, including beautiful hawk feathers found on walks in the local hills, birds' nests, a dog's skull, and a crystal ball. The pile of antique books belonged to the owner's grandfather, and the idea that they are being guarded by the carved raven is reinforced by the addition of an old key.

The Hollywood home featured in the two pictures on the left is full of curiosities. The books on display are clues to the personality and interests of their owner, a designer. A particular favorite is "Divine Decadence," which is a great source of inspiration to her. A small group of crystals lies on top of the pile for no practical purpose other than to finish the display, while A CARVED RAVEN APPEARS TO GUARD THE COLLECTION OF ANTIQUE BOOKS, WHICH HAVE ENORMOUS SENTIMENTAL VALUE.

The LA home on the right uses books in quite a different way—here, they are meant more for their original purpose of reading, maybe not intently but for picking up and flicking through the pages for ideas. THE SEEMINGLY RANDOM DISPLAY ON THE RUG-COVERED TABLE IS A CREATIVE FUSION OF THE MINDS OF ITS OWNERS.

↑ A low round coffee table covered with a richly patterned rug forms the centerpiece of this room. Piles of books, both reference and fiction, offer an enticing range of reading material to be enjoyed in the big comfy chairs.

⫸ ⫸ (NEXT PAGE) The large oval mirror hanging above the mantelpiece is from the 1920s. On close inspection, you can see that the ornate surround is a collection of vintage jewelry, which has been glued on to the original frame. Some of the brooches, bracelets, and necklaces belonged to the owner's grandmother, while others were gifts from friends. All of them have special meaning.

The large oval mirror hanging above
the mantelpiece is from the 1920s.
On close inspection, you can see
that the ornate frame is a collection
of vintage jewelry, which has been
glued on to the original frame.
There are brooches, bracelets,
necklaces, some of which belonged
to the owner's grandmother, while
others were gifts from friends. All
of them have special meaning.

◄━◄ ◄━◄ Mirrors magnify the effect of a display. Reflected in the mirrored entrance door is an assortment of framed photos of family and friends arranged on a French Art-Deco table.

◄━◄ Used as shapely bathroom storage, this barrel chest of drawers also provides the display surface for a simple gilt tray of lotions and potions. The beautiful white orchid, reflected in the carved gilt mirror, enhances the scene.

↑ Black can make a striking display. In this very well-considered hallway, the silver-framed picture of black coral and the wooden Chinese table make the perfect backdrop for the ornate carved lamp stands and wooden dishes, each one in the shape of a leaf.

A gnarled piece of an old vine has been transformed into a magnificent candle holder and now makes a bold centerpiece on the living-room table of this French home. Creating a perfect balance is the pair of metal scroll lamps with their rust finish. The wonderfully sculpted shape of the candlestick is reflected in the mirror on the right.

THE WAY WE LIVE

◄◄ ⊂ ⊃ ► An impressive Indian silver decorative table holds a carefully curated selection of treasured items, from a bronze statue in the style of Rodin to a ribbed glass vase and silver boxes.

⊌ ↓ A plain, whitewashed table has been made to look very special simply by gathering together on it decorative items all in the same color—white.

Shown together, all-white objects or all-silver, make a striking display

↑ A bronze lamp stands beside this
console table and its collection
of busts. Some were acquired at
antiques fairs and markets,
others were gifts, and one was
commissioned. Together, they are
even more impressive than they
would be separately, and the
backdrop of the formal garden,
glimpsed through the conservatory
window, adds an air of grandeur.

➡➡ This pretty collection of pitchers on the kitchen windowsill is a welcome distraction from washing the dishes! The pieces have been collected for their individual beauty but their impact is greater when displayed together. However, there is not always power in numbers, and the picture on the left shows clearly how just one striking piece, the Madonna and Child, can have the same stunning effect.

I have always been a fan of collections, which make an instant statement when presented as a theme. THE THREE STYLES OF COLLECTION SHOWN HERE ARE QUITE DIFFERENT BUT THEIR IMPACT IS EQUALLY POWERFUL.

A collection of stone and marble busts, top left, has been brought together in a conservatory and displayed on a stone console table, supported by two classical columns. The busts are diverse in style, with some majestic, others pretty, but they stand together in great harmony. The garden behind makes a lovely green backdrop and gives an almost stately-home character to the display, in contrast to the busts' casual, almost random placement.

Shown above is a very personal collection of vintage pitchers and vases, chosen for their delicate color or pattern. Gathered over the years by a designer famous for her ability to spot the perfect item, the pieces are displayed on the kitchen windowsill in her California home.

Why not TRY YOUR HAND AT STARTING A SMALL COLLECTION OF OBJECTS THAT YOU LOVE? It could be of virtually anything, and the pieces could be new, old, or retro. As you acquire the different pieces, sit them together and you will see your style emerge. It could be perfume bottles for a bathroom, pitchers for a kitchen… You may not be brave enough to collect busts but you can never be sure of where your collecting might take you.

▶ The colors in this kitchen have all been carefully chosen to complement the bright blue skies of the region—the south of France—and the pale stonework of the house. Plates, glasses, and candlesticks are reflected in the large mirror, created out of old doors bought from an antiques market. The mirrors were added to the doors at a later stage. A sweeping rusty chandelier, hanging just above the kitchen table, creates a center for the display.

THERE ARE NO REAL RULES FOR CREATING DISPLAYS IN YOUR HOME but I do think that this picture of the kitchen in an old French house is a fine example of what can be achieved through balance and pairing.

A long console table is set against one wall in front of an unusual mirror made from two old doors. Reflected in the mirror are cubbyhole shelves holding china and glass for all to see. The shelves are painted a soft duck-egg blue and set the tone for the room. The carefully chosen ginger jars and vases in shades of blue on the table are perfectly balanced, and even the plates in the foreground have a blue trim, indicating that NOTHING HERE WAS ACHIEVED BY ACCIDENT.

Flanking the display is a pair of decorative metal lamp bases with bold black shades. The striking contrast of these with the blue of the jars and vases creates an extremely pleasing tableau.

↑ Although purely for decoration, the ornamental clock looks very grand hanging on the workshop wall, and you could easily be fooled into thinking it will tell you the right time. Alongside, on the open shelves of the tall cupboard, piles of vintage fabrics have a decorative as well as practical role. Open the cupboard doors and you will discover even more fabrics collected over time. The chicken, found at an antiques fair, has no other purpose except to amuse.

← The low wooden beams, walls painted in warm tones, splashes of blue on the false door and cushions, and a pair of big comfortable sofas all come together to make a striking yet relaxing living space.

These two pictures illustrate how the use and balance of color are so important when planning a display. The room to the left is the first-floor living space of the house shown on the previous page. At the top of the stone stairs, the owner has put in a decorative false door and painted it the same duck-egg blue as the kitchen. Although in a very contrasting style to the sofa, THE METAL TABLE WITH CURVED LEGS IS IN PERFECT HARMONY WITH THE HANDRAIL AGAINST WHICH IT STANDS. Two large gilt candelabras stand on the table ready to illuminate the room with a soft glow as the sun fades.

In the LA workshop depicted above, a stuffed chicken, perched on the top shelf, adds a slightly comic touch, while piles of vintage floral fabrics, all carefully chosen for their color and pattern, adorn the open shelves beneath. THE OLD CUPBOARD, ACQUIRED AT AN AUCTION, HAS AN INTERESTING WORN CRACKLE, INDICATING A MYSTERIOUS PREVIOUS LIFE. Like everything else here, the clock has been bought for its color and finish.

←← **A strong theme runs through this kitchen** display, not only in terms of color but also in the choice of objects. Iconic representations of Native Americans—an old tin advertisement for tobacco and a ceramic ornament—as well as Mexican dolls and religious imagery feature strongly.

↑ This marble-lined bathroom and dressing room make this a dream environment. An antique Venetian mirror above the basin and curvaceous French chairs add to the feminine splendor.

The kitchen opposite shows how awe-inspiring the DISCIPLINED USE OF A FAVORITE COLOR AND THE DISPLAY OF FAVORITE OBJECTS can be. Turquoise appears in the paint on the cupboards and walls and also in the Fiesta ware china, which has been collected for its depth of color and clever match to the paintwork. Unlike the kitchen, THE UTTERLY FEMININE BATHROOM AND DRESSING ROOM HAVE A SOFT AND RELAXING FEEL but they, too, are filled with objects that have special meaning for the owner.

Give a display authenticity by creating it out of objects that have real meaning for you

◄─◄ **A wonderful mix of color and retro classics.** The red **Anglepoise** lamp and **1960s** arc lamp illuminate art by **Gilbert & George** and **Volker Stox** alongside **Vallauris** ceramics. The collection of books softens the designer look to make it more homey.

In this intriguing space, there is an abundance of images of Native Americans, both photographs and stylized representations, and also an old map of Paris, maybe reminding the owner of his European connections.

◄─◄ This is a very eclectic display, with a lot of history, but one that has been put together with a certain amount of order to create a real sense of balance. The African carving, bought at auction, used to belong to Yves Saint Laurent, who kept it in his Paris apartment. Less distinguished origins are attached to the red painting, which was, literally, found on the street in Madrid. The Ken doll was once wrapped in gold paper and presented as an "Oscar" at a party, while the Art-Deco clock belonged to the owner's grandmother.

▷─▷ The owner of this Venice Canals house in LA has a rare and distinctive style, which is abundantly evident in this remarkable display. A bold painting by the Russian artist Sveta Yavorsky, with its strong color and seemingly floating subject matter, sits above an elegant Hugues Chevalier table. Precious family photographs are the perfect finishing touch.

Both of these displays, in different homes, have real significance for their owners but they are so well considered that they also resonate with others. The pieces are not connected in any literal sense but their owners have no qualms about putting them together as a display.

These three interiors have a number of things in common but the most interesting is the oversized scale of the furniture compared to the size of the rooms. Making the rooms comfortable was the reason behind the design decisions made, as well as a desire to incorporate the large pieces of art in the space. BIG SOFT SOFAS, CUSHIONS, AND THROWS DELIVER THE REQUIRED DEGREE OF COMFORT, WHILE THEIR TEXTURES AND TONES COMPLEMENT THE PAINTINGS ON THE WALLS.

On paper, the different elements in these rooms might seem totally at odds but in reality they work incredibly well together. For example, in the picture on the right, the imposing Viramontes painting makes an unexpected but totally effective backdrop to the plaster statue of Leda and the Swan, a motif from Greek mythology, displayed appropriately on the capital of a classical-style column. Also unlikely in terms of pairing is the floor-standing iron candlestick from Mexico but its inclusion is inspired. Such eclectic elements give a home its individuality.

↑ A sense of drama is created with this idiosyncratic combination of a romantic painting by the French artist Laurence Amélie, an oversized sofa, a statue of the Madonna, and a chunky wooden crucifix.

▣➤ With the ocean the backdrop to this Malibu house and also to the painting, this work by the Italian artist Ubaldo Franceschini has found the perfect home.

▣➤ ▣➤ An imposing piece of art by Tony Viramontes, the American fashion illustrator, makes a bold statement that complements the dramatic quality of the interior.

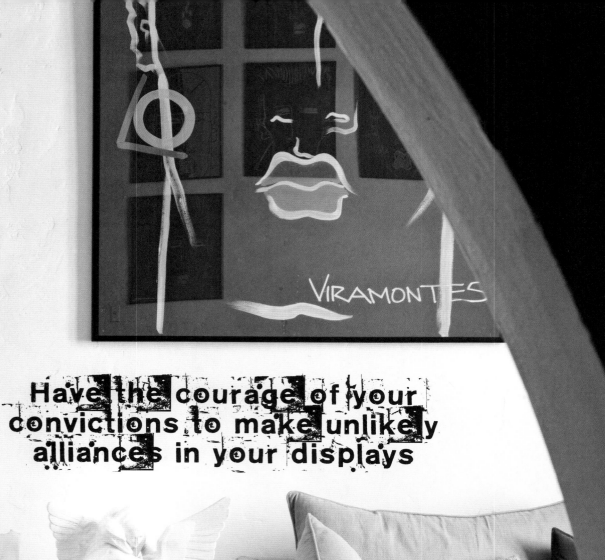

Have the courage of your convictions to make unlikely alliances in your displays

Relaxation and comfort are the overriding considerations for these rooms

The Deco-style home in Venice Canals, LA, above, is
a testament to the owners' rare gift for choosing and
marrying together beautiful pieces of furniture. In the
living room, **ALL EYES ARE ON THE UNUSUAL CENTRAL COFFEE
TABLE, WITH THE THREE SMALLER TABLES FITTING SNUGLY
BENEATH,** which are brought out when entertaining. The
deep, Deco-style armchairs surrounding it are both
comfortable and stylish, and create a perfect balance.
IN SUCH A SOPHISTICATED, NEAT SPACE, NO MORE ADORNMENT IS NEEDED THAN
THE DECO STATUE OF A DANCER. In a busy world, comfortable chairs

Nutty tones combine in soft
harmony. The high gloss of the
table and the clean lines of the
chairs exemplify this room's
immaculate and well-thought-out
design. Restrained and calming,
the room's only concession to
pattern is on the rug.

The traditional white
marble fireplace plays center
stage in this room, with the
carefully chosen accessories and
decorative ornaments completing
the scene with unique flair.

The glow from the
candles and the fireplace gives
a warm and natural ambience,
something that is rarely achieved
with such style in the Californian
climate. The clever use of vintage
finds, soft textiles, and flickering
light are testament to the design
skills of the owner.

by an open fire and piles of wonderful books are just the elements you need for relaxation. Finding the time to relax may not always be possible, but the fact that the room has been prepared is in itself reassuring.

EVERYTHING ABOUT THE SCENE ON THE RIGHT—THE ROUND 1960S BLACK MARBLE AND CHROME COFFEE TABLE, THE VASE OF FLOWERS, THE PILE OF BOOKS, AND THE DECORATIVE ITEMS ON THE MANTELPIECE—HAS BEEN CAREFULLY CONSIDERED AND PLACED TO CREATE A VERY WELL-BALANCED DISPLAY.

A big, brick-built fireplace, two inviting linen-covered fireside chairs, and a stripped wooden coffee table are the key anchors in this Santa Monica sitting room. The owner, Rachel Ashwell, knows all about comfort and has built a brand around her own particular style. HER ABILITY TO CREATE A LAID-BACK HOME WITH A REAL, INDIVIDUAL LOOK IS AN ENVIABLE AND SPECIAL GIFT.

◄━◀ The unusual occasional table in this sunny reading corner complements the stone floor and the warm colors of the chaise longue.

▶━▶ A vintage coffee table adds a real sense of individualism to this space, while the soft gray linen sofa and decorative screen make a harmonious backdrop.

▶━▶ ▶━▶ The eye is immediately drawn to this exquisite decorative lamp in etched glass on top of a Chinese lacquered wooden table.

▼ A weathered metal garden table has been brought indoors as an informal surface for displaying candles, flowers, and a treasured collection of shells and coral.

Occasional tables are vital for a comfortable life. Placed next to an armchair or in front of a sofa, they can be used to hold a lamp, place a hot drink, rest a book, show off a cherished object. HERE ARE SOME GREAT EXAMPLES OF DIFFERENT STYLES OF TABLE, HOW THEY CAN BE USED, AND HOW THEY BECOME A FOCAL POINT IN THE ROOM.

In the picture opposite, beside the chaise longue, is a very unusual occasional table. Resembling a large barrel with a metal stand on top to hold the glass, it is a decorative item in its own right. The two bowls on the table do not compete but simply reflect the carefully balanced color scheme of the room. CONVERSELY, IF AN ITEM IS OF SUFFICIENT BEAUTY, THEN IT DESERVES TO BE THE FOCUS OF ATTENTION. IN THE PICTURE ABOVE, A STUNNING ETCHED GLASS LAMP DRAWS THE EYE.

Bear in mind that occasional tables need not always be designed specifically for the role. PROVIDED IT IS FLAT AND STABLE, ALMOST ANYTHING CAN BE USED AS A SHOWCASE FOR A VARIETY OF DISPLAYS.

↑ Illuminating a display of French
neoclassical prints is a bizarre
bedside lamp with a stem of ostrich
eggshells and a shade of guinea
fowl feathers. The small glass-
topped table also holds framed
family pictures and a plant,
which contribute to this carefully
constructed decorative scheme.

◄◄ The reflection of this amazing
bedroom in the ornate oval mirror is
a display in its own right. The brave
choice of yellow toile de Jouy for
the bed makes a dramatic impact
against the pale stone of the walls.

◀━ A delightful French antique dressing table is trimmed with green. The color has formed the basis of the room's decoration: a green tin, a green vase, and a bold embroidery with green highlights hanging above the bed unite the display.

▼ On a vintage bedside table, a pink glass lamp with a lace shade creates an utterly feminine and romantic aesthetic in this Malibu beach house. Reflected in the mirror is an enchanting oil painting of a young girl, perfectly positioned on the opposite wall.

Small pieces of decorative furniture play a big role in enhancing a room

◄━ **A mix of religious and cultural references** and materials comes together to make a perfectly balanced display. Hanging from the dark gray-painted wall, the copy of a **1970s** plaster panel taken from the ceiling of Southwark Cathedral makes a suitably solid backdrop to the large Chinese bamboo and cane chest with the display of leather boxes and a stone Buddha on top.

▶━ **In this bedroom,** behind the large, ribbed, onion-shaped vase on the nightstand, designed by **Michael Reeves**, stands a gesso screen, with a wall lamp in gold leaf on metal. These elements are at perfect ease with the unusually shaped white linen headboard, resulting in a haven of well-designed masculinity.

▼ **A custom-made commode,** with an elegant, shiny lamp on top, doubles up as a bedside table. These two elements make the room feel both glamorous and highly chic.

These three well-presented spaces (the rooms above and opposite are in the same home) have each been designed with every consideration for their owners' needs and to reflect their personalities. They share the same design approach–chic and minimalist with a masculine aesthetic–and the highest quality materials have been used throughout. THESE ELEMENTS, COMBINED WITH A RESTRAINED, OFTEN MONOCHROMATIC, COLOR PALETTE, HAVE PRODUCED EXCLUSIVE, WELL-CONSIDERED SPACES, with an enviable and very well-designed decoration.

These pictures, taken in two completely different homes, share the same brave choices of color. Both homes are in California, where the **WARM CLIMATE AND INTENSE LIGHT ALLOW YOU TO BE MORE ADVENTUROUS WHEN IT COMES TO COLOR.** Unsurprisingly, because of the area's heritage, there is also a Spanish feel about both of them.

In the hall above, a turquoise hand-painted chair stands alongside a hand-painted chest, with a simple display of a pitcher of roses and a perfumed candle. In the adjacent living room, the piano provides the perfect opportunity for displaying favorite pictures collected from antiques markets. Adding a sense of grandeur and reverence is a pair of elegant candelabras. The sweeping metal stair rail in the 1920s hacienda-style apartment on the right is the backdrop for an old religious print of the Virgin of Guadeloupe. Accompanying the print on the brightly painted table are favorite memorabilia and cherished photographs.

↑ Rare vintage pictures, including a religious icon, are displayed on the piano by leaning them against the wall, making the most of a functional piece of furniture. In the hall beyond, continuing the quasi-religious theme, the hand-painted chest has an altar-like appearance. A perfumed candle burns alongside a pitcher of roses from the garden.

➤➤ Whitewashed walls and a pale cream stair carpet allow the owner to use strong colors elsewhere with confidence. Everything he collects has a strong Spanish or religious reference. The black ironwork of the railings, candle holders, and wall lantern all contribute to the look.

Although on two different continents, these rooms share the same rich, atmospheric, and laid-back style

↑ Simple elements work together to create a relaxing space. The large leather sofa with patterned cushions offers absolute comfort, while the velvet-covered ottoman ensures the drinks are never far away. Pillows in complementary colors add to the informality.

◄◄ Hundreds of books, crammed onto vibrant turquoise shelves, are waiting to be leafed through.

The photograph on the left has been taken from the mezzanine floor of a Californian, hacienda-style apartment. Peering through the 1930s ironwork chandelier, you see a space that has been put together purely for relaxation. Numerous kilim cushions add to the comfort of the two large sofas, while within arm's length, on a large Moroccan tray, are books on subjects dear to the owner.

Although similar in effect and purpose, the room above is, surprisingly, not in someone's North African home but in a restaurant-cum-bar in South London.

➤ This living-room mantelpiece is covered in an array of decorative items, including a bronze carriage clock and two pairs of bronze candlesticks that complement the finish of the concrete mantelpiece. Enhancing the display is the reflection of the garden in the glass of the print above.

Miniature traditional Dutch houses make an eye-catching decorative feature lined up on a shelf above the doors of this entrance hall.

↑ On a big oak
sideboard in the
dining room, covered
in a velvet rug, sits
a collection of well-
chosen and favored
items, linked by the
owner's favorite
color, blue.

The themes running through these three rooms are the Netherlands
and the color blue, specifically the blue used in Delft china. The
rooms are all in the London home of a Dutchman, who has surrounded
himself with reminders of his birthplace.

On a shelf running along the tops of doors in the entrance hall is a
continuous row of traditional Dutch houses in miniature. INTRICATELY
DETAILED, THE HOUSES, WHICH ORIGINALLY CONTAINED GENEVER (DUTCH
GIN), WERE GIVEN TO BUSINESS-CLASS PASSENGERS BY A DUTCH AIRLINE AS
A THANK-YOU and, over the years, the owner has amassed an impressive
collection. They make an absolutely delightful display.

The top of the sideboard in THE DINING ROOM IS COVERED WITH AN ECLECTIC MIX
OF FAVORITE OBJECTS, including two Piranesi engravings bought at London's
Portobello Market more than 20 years ago, a plate from a Swedish
dinner service but decorated in Delft blue, stag antlers, and pebbles.

On the living-room mantelpiece stands a rare bronze carriage
clock, which once belonged to the owner's aunt. Candlesticks and tiny
ornaments collected over time complete the intimate display.

↑ **Rammed into the floor-to-ceiling**
↑ **shelves, rows of books collected**
purely because of the soft pale
shades of their jackets, look almost
like wallpaper.

←◄ **There is a military angle to**
this display, with a pith helmet and
a portrait of a soldier, which takes
center stage, but the toy dinosaurs
and truck confirm that this is a
young boy's bedroom.

↑ ➤→ **The portrait of a pretty yet**
↑ **serious-looking young girl leans**
against the mirror, leaving the teddy
and a duck lamp to give this display
a more childlike feel.

Clever but simple displays add a whimsical touch to these children's bedrooms

The three different rooms pictured here are in the same house belonging to Marie-France Cohen, the owner of the Paris store "Merci," which has become the symbol of global cool! As you would expect, HER HOME IS TESTAMENT TO HER UNIQUE ABILITY TO SELECT AND DISPLAY BEAUTIFUL THINGS. When you wander from room to room, you get a sense of how passionate she is about collecting from all over the world.

The bedrooms of her grandchildren, left and above, are filled with carefully curated and relevant finds, with vintage and modern toys sitting comfortably alongside old paintings. Meanwhile, in the library, above left, there is an impressive selection of vintage books all in soft pale shades, covering entire walls, even above the door. The effect is startling.

A bold and imposing black carved fireplace is the focus of this room. Its formality is enhanced by the balanced display of two lamps and two wall sconce lights, which also draw the eye to the oil painting propped up on the mantelpiece.

▲ Flanked by a pair of lamps, the railway station-style clock face takes center stage in this skillful display. The items are there to be used, and at the same time look just right.

The kitchen and living room shown here are in the home that is featured on pages 56-7, further proof, if any were needed, of Marie-France Cohen's impeccable eye for detail. BOTH DISPLAYS ARE PRACTICAL BUT ALSO DECORATIVE. IN THE KITCHEN, THE HUGE CLOCK OVERSEES A LARGE CAST-IRON CASSEROLE DISH FLANKED BY A PAIR OF TABLE LAMPS, WITH PILES OF DISHES BENEATH—ALL THE REQUIREMENTS OF A BUSY KITCHEN WHERE ITEMS ARE IN USE EVERYDAY.

As the nights draw in, the fire is lit in the cozy living room. There is BEAUTY IN IMPERFECTION here, shown in the distressed paint finishes and vintage finds, plus A STRONG SENSE OF SYMMETRY provided by the pairs of glistening crystal wall lights, antique candlesticks, unusual lamp tables, inviting sofas, and serviceable log baskets.

This beautifully balanced fireside setting is the epitome of comfort, with the distressed paint finishes and the soft linen chairs creating just the right amount of informality.

➤➤ When the silvering in an old mirror goes misty, it is known as foxing, but the imperfection actually adds charm. Here, the mercury glass bowl on the mantelpiece complements the mirror perfectly, as do the decorative silver candlesticks against the wood-paneled walls.

◄◄ Birds—stuffed ducks and an ornate wooden birdcage—are a fitting theme for a country-house hallway. The paneled piece of art complements the scene perfectly.

▲ Stretching around all four walls above the paneled dado, an impressive handmade wallpaper by Zuber makes an elegant backdrop to an equally elegant dining room.

These two settings from the same Directoire country house in France show just how effective wall decoration can be in a display. THE EXQUISITE HANDMADE ZUBER WALLPAPER RUNS ABOVE THE PANELED DADO ON ALL FOUR WALLS, MAKING AN EYE-CATCHING SETTING FOR THE DINING ROOM. MEANWHILE, IN THE FLAGSTONE HALLWAY, AN OLD PAINTING HAS BEEN DIVIDED INTO VERTICAL SECTIONS, with each piece then framed and the painting reassembled. Treated in this innovative way, it has become a striking backdrop to the long wooden console table, on which stands an old wooden birdcage and other assorted antiques.

In both rooms, pale stone-colored walls allow the decorative panels to become THE FOCUS OF ATTENTION.

Subtlety is the key to the success of these artful display techniques

↑ Tall, well-proportioned French doors opening out onto the garden and high ceilings give this space a real sense of grandeur, while the subtle decorating style creates a soothing and relaxed atmosphere. The long, floaty curtains frame the pared-down desk display beautifully.

➤➤ The long hall table is the perfect size and style for this graceful home and just the right display feature for a well-chosen assortment of vintage finds and treasured objects.

This bedroom and hallway in different French homes are the absolute epitome of grace and elegance, with their displays correspondingly subtle and well considered. The harlequin stone floor in the picture on the right is just one of many original features that tell a story of the life of the house. THE SOMEWHAT AGED HALL TABLE MAKES A FITTING DISPLAY SURFACE FOR A COLLECTION OF PERSONAL FINDS.

In the bedroom, left, a subtle vignette has been created around the small antique desk. Favorite items are displayed on top, and it has been cleverly positioned by the tall, well-proportioned window. The soft flowing curtains and white-painted Louis XVI chair complete the picture.

↑ This is a good example of strong display.
All the elements have been chosen for their
interesting and unusual qualities. Piles of books
give height, and the wall light is positioned in just
the right place to illuminate the trio of pictures on
the wall.

⫸ The oriental flavor of this diverse display,
is created by the large bamboo chest of drawers
with a colorful figure hand-painted on one side,
and the porcelain figurines on top, partially
obscured by a large plume.

⫸ ⫸ An elaborate bronze candelabra
appears most majestic alongside a collection of
leather-bound books and a slightly battered top
hat, which give balance and height to the display.

A love of the unusual, the ability to mix
different objects, and a rare sense of eclectic
individualism shine through in these displays
in the same LA home. BOOKS ARE A GREAT TOOL
FOR CREATING STRUCTURE IN A DISPLAY, AND HERE
THESE OVERSIZED TOMES HAVE BEEN SKILLFULLY
USED AS PROPS.

The master bedroom, featured in the three photographs above, shows how effective wallpaper can be in giving character and warmth to a room. Floral wallpaper by the French company Zuber, with a soft pattern of trailing sprigs of sweet peas on A PARCHMENT-COLORED BACKGROUND, ADDS A SUBTLE FEMININITY TO THIS ROOM WITHOUT MAKING IT TOO PRETTY. IT WORKS BEAUTIFULLY WITH THE BOXED BUTTERFLIES DISPLAYED ABOVE THE PIANO AND SOFTENS THE DARK, BOLD FURNITURE.

The bedroom on the right benefits from the characterization that the wallpaper brings, making it a haven for the small children it is intended for.

The color of the lampshade in this display complements the wallpaper behind perfectly. Although thematic, the paper is not at all childish and is a well-chosen addition to room.

Subtle floral wallpaper is a lovely backdrop to the dark wood antique furniture and piano in this bedroom. It has a feminine quality, but not overly so, and balances the rather more masculine elements of the room.

↓ ➤ ➤ The neutral complementary colors chosen for this master bedroom merge together seamlessly, creating a warm and cozy display. The distressed antique furniture keeps the atmosphere informal.

IN THIS MASTER BEDROOM, SOFT HARMONIOUS COLORS—CREAM, PALE GRAY, BLUSH PINK—ARE WELL BALANCED WITH TEXTURE AND THE IMPERFECTION OF ANTIQUES. A PAIR OF VINTAGE OCTAGONAL MIRRORS EITHER SIDE OF THE BED IS A BOLD BUT SUCCESSFUL ADDITION. All the choices made here, from the soft mohair throw and cushions on the chairs, to the velvet quilted throw draped over the end of the bed and the deep-buttoned, linen-covered bed head, are carefully considered, and together they create a restful and luxurious retreat. This airy, sunny bedroom is a true haven of relaxation.

◄◄◄ The ultimate living display is found in the home of the French artist Laurence Amélie, where the pet cat chooses to rest in a rather lovely Chinese-style bowl. Art, as in Laurence's painting above the sofa, imitates nature in the vase of flowers. The subtle shades of the overall decoration are typical of Laurence's romantic style.

▷▷▷ A tall open window, on a sunny day, sets the scene for this gentle still life. On a small round table, an old teapot with a broken spout and covered in splotches of paint has become the charming color-coordinated vessel for a trailing rose picked from the garden.

🌷 This round table holds a selection of vintage mercury glass candlesticks. The dramatic painting behind makes the display altogether original.

The instinctive relaxed nature of the three homes pictured here is all down to the way their owners have made the spaces feel uncontrived. THERE ARE CHILDREN OR PETS IN THEIR LIVES, SO THERE IS NO PLACE TO BE PRECIOUS ABOUT BELONGINGS. Everything is to be enjoyed. I love the way that all three decors make you feel instantly at home.

Three different spaces with very clever display ideas give a real sense of what makes their owners tick

◄◄ ◄◄ Symmetry and order are the key to the success of this display of an antique glazed tortoise shell flanked by a pair of horn candlesticks and pyramid glass lamps from Bali.

◄◄ A designer who has a great eye for detail owns this stunning London apartment on the river. Indicative of the unique and stunning displays that he carefully curates for maximum impact is this section of hallway, with a bronze statue of a woman on horseback standing on an invisible glass plinth.

➤➤ A large, linen sofa, scattered with fake fur cushions, gives this Santa Monica interiors store the look of a relaxed sitting room in someone's home. Forming the backdrop is a pair of old glazed doors, introduced as part of the store's design. A big, leather Moroccan-style pouf has been put to good use as a coffee table.

Deception is at work in the relaxed and comfortable space on the right. Unlikely as it may seem, it forms part of an interiors store. Rachel Ashwell has designed it deliberately to look like a sitting room, to convey her sense of style and aesthetic.
CLEVER USE HAS BEEN MADE OF THE RECESSED SPACE BEHIND THE SOFA SHOWN ON THE FAR LEFT. A SHELF

CREATED FROM A PERFECTLY FITTING PIECE OF GLASS SITS ON TOP OF THE DADO RAIL, MAKING A DISCREET PLINTH FOR THE WELL-ORDERED DISPLAY.

In the apartment on the left, the visitor is stopped in his tracks by the sight of a bronze statue of a woman on horseback. Displayed on a glass plinth, it appears to be floating.

CHAPTER 2

HEART OF THE HOME

The heart of the home is the big family table. Of course, this table may not be so very big, and the family may be just one person, but it is still the hub of activity. IT IS THE WORKHORSE, USED FOR MANY DIFFERENT PURSUITS, FROM EATING MEALS AND PAYING BILLS TO SEWING AND HOMEWORK, AND IT IS CONSTANTLY BEING RE-INVENTED, when the objects used for one activity are cleared away and replaced by those of another.

Using pattern and color, designer Donna Walker has customized an unremarkable mid-20th-century table, chairs, and a sideboard, making them unique and desirable.

Chosen both for its beauty and warm tones, the custom-made dining table by Peter Alexander at the heart of this LA home, left, is made of solid maple with a sycamore veneer. In complementary tones are the Tom Charnock chairs, with cashmere covers. THE STRIKING PIECE OF ART, REMINISCENT OF A TRIPTYCH, IS BY RUSSIAN PAINTER TIMUR D'VATZ. ILLUMINATING THE SCENE IS A MODERN TAKE ON A CHANDELIER IN BRONZED STEEL.

When you peer through the archway in the 1920s Californian apartment in the picture on the right, you are met with a delightful, personal scene. Warm yellow walls set off the plain dining table and chairs. The owner sits here to have his meals, as well as do some daily tasks. The colors and mixed cultures represented in the room are indicative of his style and interests.

The owners of both these homes are true to their individual styles. The rooms have different cultural references, but are striking for their bold color choice and decoration. I love the fact that they both proclaim their unique and carefully thought-out design.

◄ Like everything else in this room, the tulips have been chosen with great care and thought, and are the absolutely perfect color match.

⬇ This harmonious display of objects from different cultures and in different styles is bathed in a gentle, filtered light.

The wooden folding
screen, painted by a
contemporary Japanese
artist, establishes the
predominantly oriental
feel of this dining space.
Unusual japanned Queen
Anne chairs flank the
chunky, white-lacquered
dining table, where the
owner is about to take
tea served from a 1960s
Spode teapot. Pink roses
in a glass vase inject color
and give balance to this
graphic setting.

A weathered old table is dressed up for a special occasion. Garden flowers tied to the chair backs with string add to the rustic charm.

◄◄ **Modernism** meets country in this uncluttered, tranquil space.

These two spaces in the same converted barn in France display the owners' love of mixed styles. THE MODERNIST TABLE AND CHAIRS ON THE LEFT ARE IN STARK CONTRAST TO THE PALE STONE WALLS AND PASTORAL FEEL OF THEIR SETTING. THE OTHER TABLE, WORN AND UNREFINED, IS SET FOR A CELEBRATION LUNCH. Decorative touches, such as a candelabra, add to the sense of occasion.

Simple decorating styles allow the natural beauty of stone to shine through

◄━ This is a fine example of a well-ordered display. On top of the **1940**s dining table is a pair of mercury glass candlesticks, and behind them a pair of wooden columns, displaying matching ostrich eggs in glass vases. It is hard to imagine that the table is used as a work desk day to day.

♀ There is a real sense of humor is at work ♀ here. The large, modern, oval dining table is used for both dinner parties and as a desk, but note the plastic soldier creeping across the table, and the rubber boot on the side doubling up as a vase.

▭► The table at the center of this well-designed kitchen/dining room has an unusual combination of cast-bronze base and glass top, typical of its owners' style. The wall painting, made up of individual panels, is by Tony Barone.

This trio of well-thought-out and formal living and dining spaces in three separate homes from LA to West London shows very distinct styles of display using quite different techniques. FOR ALL OF THEM, THOUGH, THE UTMOST CARE HAS BEEN TAKEN IN CHOOSING COLORS AND IN BALANCING AND MATCHING OBJECTS. WHETHER YOUR CHOICE OF STYLE IS MATCHING OR RANDOM, THERE ARE NO PRESCRIBED RULES TO FOLLOW. If a display works for you, then just go for it! The result, as seen here, can be awesome!

Many languid hours are spent at this kitchen table in the south of France, eating and chatting in the utmost comfort, not to mention style. This is the hub of the home, and the kitchen has been designed with that in mind. The upholstered sofa, bench, and armchairs invite relaxation, so that no one feels inclined to move. Covered in a crisp white tablecloth, with off-white china and bone-handled cutlery, all ready for breakfast, the table is perfectly balanced with the soft green Paisley design of the upholstery and the duck-egg-blue of the paintwork. The look is altogether soothing and fresh.

When you enter Rachel Ashwell's beachside house in Malibu, you are immediately struck by its simple, relaxed beauty. The look appears effortless but that is the deception. Rachel takes great care to choose pieces of furniture with a worn patina or subtle colors, and soft worn linen tablecloths and mismatched vintage glasses and china. Together, items that have had a previous life go to make up a home with a heart.

A beautiful crystal chandelier hangs so low that the glass drops become part of this delectable table dressing in Rachel Ashwell's Santa Monica home. The table is set for an informal summer lunch, and all the elements have been carefully chosen to suit the occasion. The coloring is restrained, with just the soft shades of mauve, lilac, and pink featuring in the flowers, glassware, and linen napkins. The flower displays are discreet and informal, with mixed bunches from the garden filling small, vintage china pitchers.

◄◄ The relaxed atmosphere at this informal
supper has been easily achieved with the casual
mismatch of candlesticks, glasses, and chairs.
As the light fades, the room takes on a romantic
atmosphere. Flickering candlelight reflected in
the crystal chandelier adds to the magic of the
display, while flowers placed in a ceramic pitcher
are the perfect finishing touch.

▲ Humor is the order of the day with this table
display. In shades of orange, this "vegetarian
banquet," complete with a chunky ceramic
rabbit that has various body parts molded as
vegetables, would put a smile on anyone's face!

▼ (NEXT PAGE) Lunch is about to be served
in this French kitchen, featured earlier at
breakfast time on pages 88–9. The approach to
the display is slightly different here. Instead of
being covered with a cloth, the bronze tabletop
has been left bare, highlighting the pale turquoise
plates perfectly.

▲ A blue-and-white checked
tablecloth, complementary napkins,
and bone-handled knives, are the
bare essentials for this lunch setting.
Adding a touch of whimsy is a child's
pair of vintage Dutch clogs at the
place setting.

The Dutch owner of this house, also featured on pages 54–5,
is an avid collector of vintage clogs. Blue, particularly
DELFT BLUE, IS HIS FAVORITE COLOR, REMINDING HIM OF HIS
BIRTHPLACE, and he has chosen it for the milk pitcher, sugar
bowl, and tablecloth. THE BROWN WOODEN CLOGS MARCHING ACROSS
THE TABLE COMPLEMENT THE BLUE AND ARE AN AMUSING AND AFFECTIONATE
ADDITION TO THE TABLE.

I have always been a great believer in following your instincts when it comes to display and decoration, and I admire this owner's innate passion for his heritage and his sense of humor. **DON'T BE DICTATED TO BY FASHION AND ALWAYS KEEP YOUR MIND OPEN TO NEW IDEAS.** Above all, make choices that you can happily live with and enjoy day in, day out.

↑ The light in this dining room has been fused by the opaque shades at the windows. A selection of souvenirs sits on the windowsill, but in pride of place, marching across the table, is the owner's treasured collection of vintage wooden clogs.

Using white as the overall theme has given a purity to this dining space, making it striking, calm, and very relaxing. The gentle curves of the large oval table and the chairs, both design classics, suit the space and the owners' aesthetic perfectly. The still-life painting in neutral tones injects warmth, as do the chair cushions and tiled floor.

⬆ The colored panels of this Plexiglas table can be interchanged to vary the color combination and composition, as well as the kaleidoscopic effects on the surrounding walls.

➤➤ This black walnut dining table, designed by David Ling, is twenty-six feet long, with a ten-foot dining section. Red-upholstered chairs complement the space well and ensure complete comfort in this family home.

These photographs are of two modern loft spaces in
different New York homes, where tables are the immediate
focus of attention. THE PLEXIGLAS TABLE FEATURED ABOVE
HAS BEEN DESIGNED BY JONNY DETIGER FOR HIS OWN HOME. IT
IS AN INTRIGUING PIECE BUT ALSO PRACTICAL, WITH MANY FAMILY MEALS HELD
AROUND IT. Light enters the apartment at different angles at
different times of the day and, while passing through the
Plexiglas, it projects a kaleidoscope of rays onto the
walls, bringing about subtle color changes to the room.

In the dining room seen on the left, a remarkable walnut
table designed by US-based Chinese architect David Ling is
the center of attention. Twenty-six feet long, this ten-
foot dining section serves as the multifunctional hub of
the home. Used for meals, homework, school projects,
or simply surfing the web, IT IS QUITE SIMPLY THE FAMILY
WORKHORSE and a perfect example of how good design can
satisfy the practical needs of a family.

Design meets function in this dazzling French country home

⬆ Two dark green enamel lamp shades hang low over the dining table, their color suiting the rustic style of the kitchen. **A** generous vase of flowers, picked from the garden, adds just the right decorative touch. The windows have been thrown open to let the early fall sun stream through and bring life to this glorious space.

➡➡ **A** row of pots and pans hanging from the wall, a large stew pot, and a set of weighing scales are all neatly stored in this compact and functional space, to make life easier for the cook.

In Marie-France Cohen's home just outside Paris, we once again witness her incredible talent for design and decoration (see also her rooms on pages 56~7 and 60~1). She has made her kitchen, that most functional of rooms, a pleasure to be in and a place to linger. THINKING FIRST AND FOREMOST OF HER FAMILY, WHO WILL SIT DOWN TO ENJOY THEIR MEALS, SHE HAS GIVEN CENTER STAGE TO THE LARGE WOODEN TABLE.

A grand old clock hangs above a side table, decorative as well as practical, as are the cast-iron dish beneath, the lamp, and the collection of dishes and bowls, all ready to be used. The highchair set at one end of the table welcomes a small grandchild to join the adults. EVERYTHING HERE HAS BEEN PUT TOGETHER WITH A SUBTLE AND SYMPATHETIC EYE, TOTALLY IN KEEPING WITH THE TRADITIONAL CHARM OF THE HOUSE.

THE ROOM SEEN BELOW, JUST OFF THE MAIN KITCHEN, WAS ONCE THE FOOD AND COOKING STORE. Now, it provides a home for the pots and pans, hung from metal hooks above the old shallow stone sink, and useful storage for fruit and vegetables brought in fresh from the local market.

A magnificent dining room comes to life with this remarkable Zuber wallpaper. Handmade and painted in strong colors, it depicts a vibrant 18th-century pastoral scene. In contrast, the actual dining style appears quite modest.

◄◄ Above the kitchen work surface hangs a rather bold abstract painting by Ubaldo. The brushed steel appliances are an incongruous but fitting match with this striking piece of art.

►► In spite of hectic schedules, care is always taken over presentation. Set for breakfast, the well-dressed kitchen table displays a delectable feast, with elegant cakestands for cheese and fruit, matching mugs of coffee, and various holders for the boiled eggs.

◄◄ To the left of the stove, a silver jug of flowers and a pretty table lamp, presided over by another abstract painting by Ubaldo, show how a functional kitchen can also be decorative.

A well-designed, modern kitchen sits alongside the art created by its owners

These three pictures are of the same kitchen in the home just outside Paris of two artists, Laurence Amélie and Ubaldo Franceschini, and their children. IT COMES AS NO SURPRISE THAT THE COUPLE'S PAINTINGS ARE HANGING THROUGHOUT THE HOUSE. EVEN THE KITCHEN HIGHLIGHTS THEIR CREATIVE ENERGY AND ARTISTIC VISION. But the room is much more than a picture gallery. For such a busy couple,

IT IS ESPECIALLY IMPORTANT FOR THE KITCHEN TO BE PRACTICAL AND TO WORK EFFICIENTLY, BUT IT MUST ALSO BE COMFORTABLE AND AESTHETICALLY PLEASING. This they have achieved apparently without effort, neatly combining function with art. Three crystal-drop chandeliers hanging over the table provide the unexpected finishing touches, combined with the beautiful French linen.

A fusion of cultures is on show in the West London home of an artist and photographer couple, shown just below and right. THE ELABORATELY CARVED WOODEN ARCHWAY FROM THE DINING ROOM THROUGH TO THE CONSERVATORY HAS AN INDIAN HERITAGE, WHILE THE BLUE LAMPS AND TABLECLOTHS, AS WELL AS THE WOODEN BENCH SEAT, TAKE THEIR CUE FROM NORTHERN EUROPE. This is a delightful dining space,

↑ The art above the dining table is impeccably hung, balancing perfectly with the low-hanging lamps which are color-matched to the room. The blue bench seat contrasts with the carved dining chairs that surround the blue-decorated table.

practical for family meals but also stylish and eclectic. The art on the wall is well balanced. All the pieces have been chosen to complement one another. A pitcher of oversized sunflowers from the garden adds to the informal but urbane charm.

The picture below right shows an equally delightful table set for a child's breakfast. THE ORIGINAL FLOOR TILES OF THIS PARIS HOME MAKE A GORGEOUS BACKDROP TO A RANDOM SELECTION OF VINTAGE CHAIRS, INCLUDING A SMALL CHILD'S CHAIR, SURROUNDING THE ROUND, TIMEWORN TABLE.

The dining area opens onto the conservatory, and light filters through the carved archway. Subtle shades of blue and green give the room a calm and relaxed feeling, punctuated by the bowl of bright sunflowers.

This table setting shows how style does not have to be compromised just because you have children. The dining table, viewed from above, has been set for breakfast. The delightful child's eggcup and china are both vintage finds.

CHAPTER 3
WORK SPACES

↑ ←◀ These two photos represent the creative hub in separate locations of a truly inspiring designer, Rachel Ashwell. Both are private spaces where she can immerse herself in the pictures, photos, and colors of her world. A sketch found in a flea market could inspire a piece of furniture, while a snip of fabric could be reproduced to create a new line of bed linen. Although small, these details speak volumes to her. Pinned to a board, they are reminders and ideas that can be used in her designs at a later date, while pictures of loved ones simply make her smile.

While researching this book, I was lucky enough to meet some very interesting and talented people who kindly let me photograph their work spaces. These ranged from a studio shared with like-minded artists to a room in a house, even a barn. The tools of their trades included paintbrushes and knives, a computer, or just a simple pen. THESE PEOPLE ALL SURROUNDED THEMSELVES WITH OBJECTS THAT, FOR THEM, WERE THE SOURCE OF THEIR INSPIRATION, NO MATTER HOW BIZARRE. WORKING IN THE CREATIVE WORLD CAN BE LONELY AT TIMES, so a work space that is comfortable and personal is as important as having all the right components to do the task at hand. ONLY THEN IS THE MIND TRULY FREE TO WANDER AND THINK BLISSFULLY OF THE NEXT BIG THING.

➤➤ In an old warehouse, large
bolts of various fabrics wait to be
cut and turned into curtains on a
simple draper's table. On the wall,
the large oil painting of a woman
in black oversees the creative
activity below. The curvaceous
vintage lamp has two shades ready
to illuminate the table when the
light starts to fade. Even though
this is a working space, the scene
is a striking still life, filled with
color, texture, and charm.

◄◄ A divine house near Venice Beach is the home as well as work space of a young fashion designer. To get to work, she just has to walk from her bedroom into this creative space, where she immerses herself immediately in her craft. The light and airy room speaks volumes about her world of fashion and is filled with all the elements that she finds inspiring. She can spend hours drawing and thinking of her next creations at the large and weathered table. By the wall, and reflected in the beautiful carved vintage mirror, is an old tailor's dummy, ready for pinning with new designs, which helps to establish a sense of color and proportion. Rails of vintage clothes are reflected in the modern, floor-to-ceiling mirror. These elements are not only practical and inspirational but also decoration for the space.

Full of character, this work space in is the creative center for a talented young designer

Surrounded by windows, which allow the space to be filed with light, this is the studio of a renowned candle designer–a room in a little wooden house that she calls her witch's cottage. It was built in the 1900s and ITS SETTING IS IDYLLIC, NESTLED AT THE BASE OF THE HOLLYWOOD HILLS, RIGHT BELOW THE FAMOUS "HOLLYWOOD" SIGN, AND WITH BREATHTAKING VIEWS OF THE CANYON BELOW. The wooden, folding art table, which once belonged to her artist father, forms the heart of her working life. Decades olds, it is a beautiful piece of furniture in its own right.

◄ The creative world of this designer revolves around her desk. This very precious piece of furniture belonged to her father, an artist, and in itself never fails to inspire her. The large, majestic candle holder to the left of the picture is a vintage find from Mexico and the perfect platform for displaying one of her creations.

► An ordered display of treasured and beautiful images—picture postcards, magazine cuttings, even notes from friends—pinned to the wall is an enduring piece of inspiration. The antique brass lamp, with its seductive curves, is practical as well as good-looking.

Giant abstract oil paintings leaning
against the walls of this barn in the
countryside outside LA are all the
work of the Italian artist Ubaldo
Franceschini. The bicycle is not
as incongruous as it might appear.
The fresh air and sunshine of this
beautiful area are a constant
source of inspiration, so jumping
on the bike and pedaling off allows
him to capture the colors of his
surroundings in his work, as well
as giving him physical exercise.

The dreamy quality of this picture conjures up the magical nature of the work of the French artist Laurence Amélie. Transformed into a tablecloth after weeks of painting, the paint-spattered plastic floor covering has the random quality of something achieved by sheer accident. The addition of the wildflowers indicates how important nature is to the artist when painting those exquisite ballerina dresses.

Provocative words as well as images inform this artist's playful approach to her work

◄── **A comfortable chair and an ordered desk,** combined with an idiosyncratic wall display, are characteristic of a hard-working artist, who works in an environment that suits her creativity perfectly.

▷─► **A page of a sketch book lies open on the** desk. The book contains a mix of drawings of people in the public eye and those not famous at all, pointing to the artist's need to draw reference from the world around her. Two examples of her paper art sit side by side, each testament to her incredible skill.

Although small, the work space of artist Abigail Aked contains everything she needs for both the practical and the creative aspects of her work in visual imagery and origami. To one side is a tall and functional shelf unit containing work files and many reference books, topped with pots of paintbrushes and other equipment. HER APPROACH TO HER WORK IS PLAYFUL, SOMETIMES IRREVERENT, WHICH IS REFLECTED IN HER CHOICE OF FOUND PRINT COVERING THE WALL IN FRONT OF THE DESK. CUT-OUTS AND QUOTES, SOME OF A PROVOCATIVE NATURE, ARE ALL IDEAS AND INSPIRATIONS FOR HER EVER-CHANGING AND THOUGHTFUL DESIGNS. They fuel her desire to experiment with printed matter and discover new ways in which to make collages and geometric shapes in art.

For a hair and make-up artist, there couldn't be a better work space. Backed by a vast mirror, the dressing table is bathed in light, with all the tools of her trade in clear view.

This cramped and jumbled space in East London belongs to an installation artist who works mostly with psychological themes. HER INSTALLATIONS ARE INCREDIBLY POWERFUL, ALWAYS THOUGHT-PROVOKING, AND SOMETIMES VERY DISTURBING. Here, you can catch a glimpse of the creative process behind them. MANY OF THE OBJECTS HERE TRIGGER IDEAS, AS WELL AS PUTTING FORWARD UNCONVENTIONAL VIEWS. Piles of books for reference, a doll's head, and high-tech accessories sit juxtaposed with written and typed statements that challenge, pictures that provoke, and old and disused elements. They all pull together to help feed the artist's imagination.

A rich and demanding environment, sometimes disturbing but never dull

A doll's head looks almost macabre, perched on top of a laptop and a notebook filled with jottings and sketches.

It is difficult to see where the artist could sit in this chaotic space, but a sense of order does exist. Everything has a potential use—old machinery, discarded typewriters, boxes, and papers, all prompting creative ideas and techniques, are here to be used in future installations.

A glimpse into the world of a busy artist reveals letters, papers, books, an old desk lamp, and scribbled notes to remind her of various important tasks.

Two rows of unframed stills behind an independent film director's desk puncture this monochromatic and relaxed space. The diverse images give a rare glimpse into her working world and the stuffed deer's head makes a puzzling but striking addition to the display.

Margaret Howell

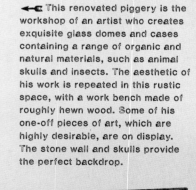

◄─◙ This renovated piggery is the workshop of an artist who creates exquisite glass domes and cases containing a range of organic and natural materials, such as animal skulls and insects. The aesthetic of his work is repeated in this rustic space, with a work bench made of roughly hewn wood. Some of his one-off pieces of art, which are highly desirable, are on display. The stone wall and skulls provide the perfect backdrop.

⬅️◄ When seated at her desk, this artist has everything to hand to enable her to design her beautiful pieces of origami.

The beautiful work here is by artist **Oana Camilleri**. Her paintings have a clear and defined style, just like her work space—well ordered and neat.

The very ordered studio of an
artist/designer who is methodical
and whose work requires very
few tools, hence the neatness
of the space.

⬆⬆ The briefcase on this desk, and its
⬆⬆ contents, symbolize a make-believe
business. A complete installation, this was
created by the designer for a recent exhibition.

➤➤ Two computer-generated images
representative of this artist's work, a red pot
containing pencils and pens, and a few rough
sketches all show signs of work in progress.

Simplicity is key to this studio
space. A plain wooden desk and a white
plastic chair are the only pieces of
furniture needed by artist/designer
Alex Starck, while a pristine WHITE
PC AND KEYBOARD ARE THE ONLY REAL TOOLS
NECESSARY FOR HIM TO NAVIGATE HIS ARTISTIC
ADVENTURE. HIS ART IS STRIKING AND

TENDS TO BE ON THE DARK SIDE, BUT
THE COLORFUL COMPUTER-GENERATED IMAGES ON
THE WALL AND DESK GIVE THE SPACE A PLAYFUL,
POP-ART FEEL. A clamp-on metal desk
lamp, a few pens, and a cutting board
hint at the intricate processes that
take place during the development of
his work.

A sun-filled, third-floor room is the home studio of dress designer Ian Wallace, in the throes of designing gowns for flamboyant entertainers. The practical tasks of cutting and sewing take place here but so, too, does the initial creativity. He has a very clear vision of the direction in which he wants to take his designs, and he surrounds himself with those things from which he can draw inspiration. The looming print of Damien Hirst's jeweled skull "For the Love of God" and several other skull references are among them.

FOR THE LOVE of GOD

The vivid and magpie imagination of this clothes designer is apparent everywhere you look in his studio, which is seen from a different angle on the previous page. A large, upside-down triangle hanging on the wall is used for storing the colorful threads that he uses every day, while on the shelf above stands the white figurine of a cartoon character. An ornate heart-shaped mirror adds a touch of vintage glamour to the space.

SOMETIMES, JUST BECAUSE OF THE NATURE OF YOUR WORK, BEAUTY IS CREATED BY ACCIDENT, AND IT IS THE UNEXPECTED AND THE IMPERFECT THAT ARE SO APPEALING. THE ARTIST LAURENCE AMÉLIE EMBRACES THE ART CREATED BY THE PAINT SPLASHES SHE MAKES AS SHE WORKS. Her pots start life as purely practical containers for her brushes but then take on an artistic role themselves, covered in Laurence's trademark colors that she uses for her painting. Laurence has a delicate hand with color, fusing it with nature, as shown in these paintings of flowers on the right. Her paintings of tutus, one of her favorite themes, are equally romantic and appealing.

THE LOCATION OF THE WORK SPACE ON THE LEFT, A CHATEAU IN PARIS, COULDN'T BE GRANDER BUT THE DESK IS SIMPLICITY ITSELF. As the owner sets to work, all her practical needs are met by her notebooks and something to write with. But what makes the space so appealing is the vase of green hydrangeas and the lustrous coffee cup and milk pitcher in an equally vivid turquoise.

◄◄ The beauty of imperfection is clear to see in this Parisian château. Peeling wallpaper and the worn and dilapidated woodwork create a rare beauty and are a gracious backdrop to a simple working space.

▶▶ The studio of the artist Laurence Amélie is covered in random splashes of paint, pots of brushes, and unfinished work. Her pots are symbolic of her style, although they have been created by sheer accident.

➤➤ At the top of the house, overlooking the street below, is this well-organized and tidy work space of a photographer/clothes designer. A selection of favorite found objects, all of them inspirational in their own way, line the windowsill, while a piece of vintage linen lies on the desk. Photographs of loved ones are an appropriate addition to this deeply personal work space.

inspire ... and smile ...

↑ ←◼ This is a really clever selection of recycling ideas. Under the glass top of a coffee table, a random selection of Scrabble letters has been inserted and used as decoration, while under another, there is a collection of envelopes, mailed from all over the world—real conversation pieces. The third picture is of the table shown in the detail above.

←◼ The coffee table with envelopes inserted under the glass is shown here in its setting.

↑ Black-and-white photographs from a memorable birthday have been stuck onto foam board, then placed under the glass top of a metal coffee table. Flipping over the board to show a different set of pictures allows you to relive another special occasion.

UPCYCLING

CHAPTER 4

For those puzzled by the word, upcycling simply means converting a waste or disposed-of item into something of higher quality and value and of practical use. ITS CLOSE RELATIVE, RECYCLING, IS A WAY OF PROCESSING SOMETHING USED, for example, turning a trunk into a coffee table, an old door into a table-the list is endless.

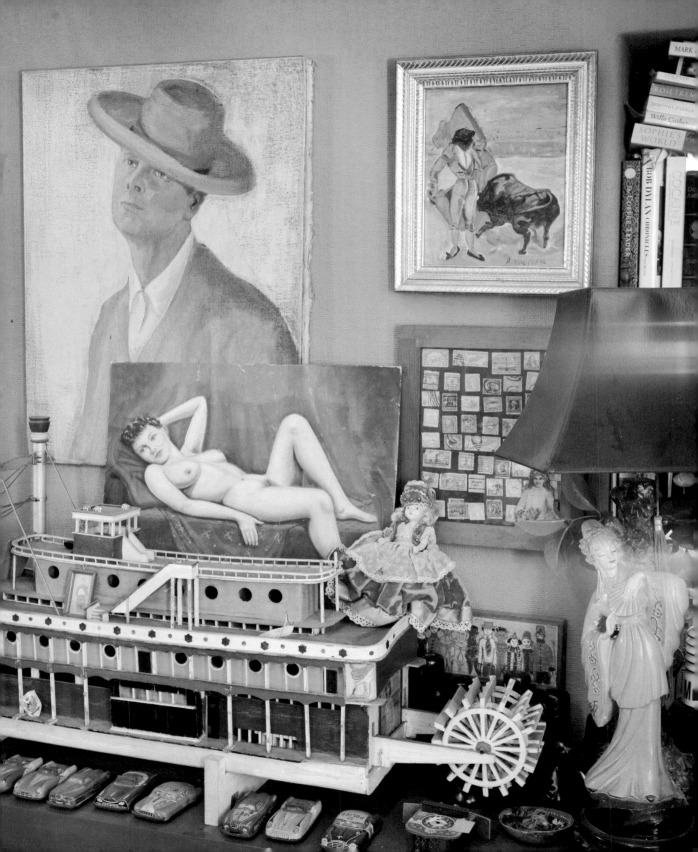

◄◄ Nothing in this study has really been recycled but the decorative objects have all lived lives elsewhere and have their own history. The paintings have hung on walls in other homes, perhaps other countries, while the vintage toy cars and the paddle steamer bear the scars of playtime going back many years.

▷▷ No longer used for playing records, a sturdy **1920**s gramophone player has been given a new lease of life as a display surface for a rather grand ormolu clock and a Georgian silver tea service.

▽ A tall and rusty radiator cover, with a slab of marble laid on top, becomes an impressive plinth for a big glass bowl of shells.

These pictures illustrate just a few of the many uses that can be given to objects that started life with an altogether different purpose. THEY ALL HAVE A STORY TO TELL BUT NOW THEY ARE MOVING ON TO A DIFFERENT LIFE SO THEIR STORIES WILL CHANGE. My journey through friends' homes, being amazed by their imaginative re-use of objects, has really taught me to be open-minded. TRY TO LOOK AT THINGS WITH FRESH EYES AND FROM DIFFERENT POINTS OF VIEW. YOU NEVER KNOW WHAT YOU MIGHT FIND.

◄◄◀ This young designer's home is a showcase of his creative skills. A discarded vinyl LP has been re-invented as the top of a side table, while an old cine camera has been adapted to become a desk lamp. Clever, inventive, and, above all, stylish.

▶▶▶ These bellows from a foundry have needed no adaptation to take on a different but still practical role as a coffee table. Their dark, rich leather sits comfortably with the modern, upholstered sofa, and gives the room a truly individual look.

Large hand bellows have, rather fittingly, been re-incarnated as a fireside coffee table in this cozy living room, and look almost as if they are blowing life into the fire. THE FOLDED LEATHER OF THE BELLOWS' CHAMBER AND THE HARD, SHINY SURFACE MAKE A GOOD-LOOKING, SOLID TABLE THAT IS PERFECTLY AT EASE HERE.

IN CONTRAST, THERE IS NOTHING PARTICULARLY FITTING ABOUT THE ORIGIN OF THE LONG METAL TABLE ON THE RIGHT—it was once used in a hospital for examinations. However, its original use is of no consequence, especially as IT NOW HAS A FABULOUS NEW LIFE HOLDING AN ECLECTIC MIX OF CAREFULLY CHOSEN ART AND POTS.

THE OWNERS OF THESE TWO HOMES HAVE TAKEN A GAMBLE BY INTRODUCING THESE UNLIKELY RECYCLED PIECES but it has really paid off. The rich, dark colors, styles, and finishes of the rooms are actually enhanced by them. Both displays say to me, "BE BRAVE AND TAKE A CHANCE."

↑ A fairly plain fire surround, a big basket of logs, and a roaring fire are the setting for a coffee table created from huge leather bellows. What a clever idea! Next time you are at an antiques market, take a second look around you. What an object is now and what it could be are two different things.

➔ This is a daring piece of recycling. A hospital examination table from the 1900s has become the base of a bold display, showing a selection of ceramic and earthenware vases in moody earth tones, a Burmese Buddha made of stone, and a large piece of multimedia art.

Rescued from a French barn undergoing renovation, this exterior door now has a brand new purpose in life. Its faded, weatherbeaten colors perfectly complement the pale flagstone floor.

The term "recycled" often suggests something utilitarian and practical, but here are two examples of what can be achieved with a little imagination. ALL IT TAKES IS TO LOOK AT SOMETHING WITH A FRESH EYE—FORGET ITS ORIGINAL USE AND EXPLORE ITS NEW POSSIBILITIES.

This wooden French door is a great example of how something old can be adapted for another everyday purpose. Supported by cinder blocks set at an angle, it makes a perfect coffee table, ITS RUSTED HINGES AND METAL STUDS ADDING TO ITS INTRINSIC BEAUTY. THE ATTRACTIVE WOOD AND METAL TRUNK, LEFT, IS NOW EMPLOYED TO PROVIDE USEFUL STORAGE, BUT IT COMES WITH A SENSE OF HISTORY AND ADVENTURE. It looks both masculine and sophisticated in a living-room setting.

◄━ ➤► I always knew that the magazines I had collected over the years would be put to good use! Stacked in neat piles with a heavy piece of glass on top, they make a highly original and personal side table. The vase of white tulips, the white porcelain bowl, and the painting leaning against the wall literally top off the display.

Most of us collect magazines or, at least, never get around to throwing them out. What better way to upcycle them than by turning them into a table? I SIMPLY TOOK A HUGE PILE OF MY FAVORITE HOME DESIGN MAGAZINES, DIVIDED THEM INTO SIX EQUAL PILES, AND STACKED THEM TOGETHER NEATLY. I THEN LAID A MADE-TO-MEASURE PIECE OF GLASS WITH SMOOTHED EDGES OVER THE TOP. Deciding on which magazines to put on the top of each pile took a long time, as they needed to fit in with the color and style of the rest of the room. Should the decoration of the room change, it couldn't be simpler to replace the top magazines for a totally different look.

Make something useful and original from old magazines by turning them into a side table

■➤ Ceramic tiles in orange, black, and white, laid out in a Mondrian-style pattern, make a striking, retro-inspired coffee table.

A colorful selection of ingenious recycling ideas using different materials

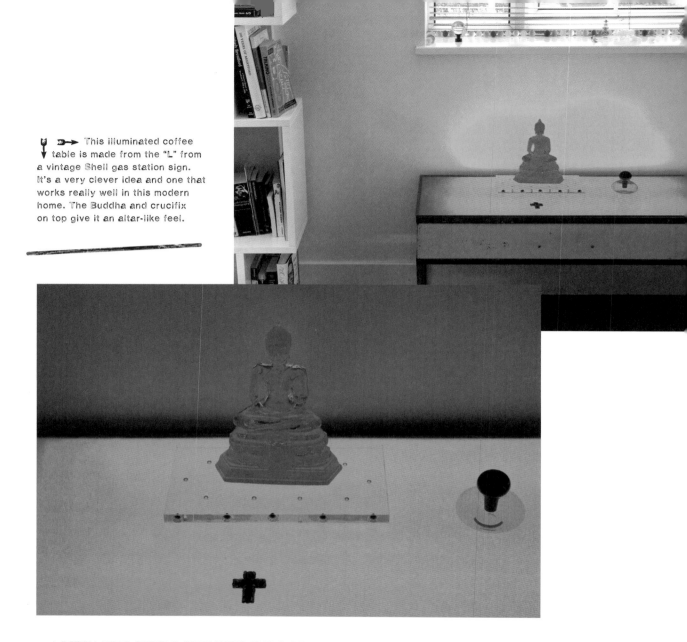

This illuminated coffee table is made from the "L" from a vintage Shell gas station sign. It's a very clever idea and one that works really well in this modern home. The Buddha and crucifix on top give it an altar-like feel.

I OFTEN HEAR PEOPLE BEMOANING THE FACT THAT THEY CAN'T FIND A COFFEE TABLE THEY LIKE. But it shouldn't be difficult at all. There are lots of ideas in this book, as these pictures show. WITH A LITTLE IMAGINATION, YOU CAN ADAPT AN EXISTING TABLE OR TURN SOMETHING UNUSUAL THAT YOU'VE DISCOVERED AT AN ANTIQUES FAIR OR IN A FLEA MARKET OR JUNK STORE INTO A PIECE OF FURNITURE THAT WILL SUIT YOUR HOME PERFECTLY.

REMEMBER, A COFFEE TABLE IS SIMPLY A TABLE WITH SHORT LEGS, SO ALL YOU REALLY NEED IS A SAW! Although, having said that, there is a rare skill involved in achieving legs that are all the same length!

▶▶ In this one picture, there are several examples of the creativity and imagination of young, London-based designer **Adam Towner.** An old work bench, cleaned and varnished, surrounded by sturdy dining chairs, long past their prime, and leather-topped stools, has become the setting for a formal afternoon tea. Lining the walls are old doors, which have been sawn in half to fit the space. Brioches have been laid out on cake stands made from discarded vinyl records, making an unlikely alliance with the mismatching vintage china. **A**ll these elements combine to give the space a truly original feel. **O**ther examples of this creative mind at work are on pages **144, 148,** and **163.**

The ingenious coffee table shown below came about purely by accident. It is made up of a packing crate of pressed chipboard, which originally held some kitchen doors delivered when the family was renovating their home. AS THEY HAD NO FURNITURE AT THE TIME, THEY USED THE CRATE AS A MAKESHIFT COFFEE TABLE, BUT THEN GREW TO LOVE IT, ESPECIALLY AS THEIR NAME AND ADDRESS ARE WRITTEN ON THE SIDE, TOGETHER WITH A "HANDLE WITH CARE" LABEL. The simplicity of design and the modest materials complement this loft space particularly well and also suit the enormous, comfortable seating modules.

In the picture on the right, the slouchy, natural linen sofas are complemented by a rather battered old leather trunk that has been recycled as a coffee table. It also makes excellent storage for books and magazines, as well as a giant footstool. It is both sturdy and functional, and

↓ A disused packing crate has been adapted for use as a coffee table, and now makes a wonderful centerpiece in this New York loft space. The delivery address and the "handle with care" label are still attached from the time the crate was delivered, which only add to its charm.

Two different takes on a coffee table but both great examples of recycling

⬆ **A well-traveled leather trunk with** **signs of wear has taken on a less demanding role as a coffee table. It is also very useful as storage for magazines and newspapers, and as a footstool.**

because leather looks great mixed with natural linen, TRUNKS AND SUITCASES IN ALL MATERIALS MAKE GREAT SIDE TABLES AND COFFEE TABLES. They require no adjustment and no remodeling. See the photo on page 162, too, which illustrates the effective use of something very decorative. That bottom trunk clearly had a previous life and probably traveled extensively around the globe, giving it an even greater story than most recycled products.

← What an ingenious and attractive bedside table, made up of one travel chest stacked on top of another. Together, they create just the right height for the rather high bed, and also provide extra storage.

Here is another example of a clever idea by Adam Towner, whose work is also featured on pages **144, 148,** and **158–9.** An ordinary gray metal locker, tipped onto its side and with legs added, has been turned into a sideboard, with useful pull-up cupboards.

Beneath the glass top of this amazing table created by Giuseppe Romeo is a collection of black and cream sculpted pieces. The table's design is both daring and brilliant, and it takes a strong creative fusion of minds to live with and enjoy such a distinct piece of furniture.

These pictures are from the extraordinary apartment of the artists and designers Rodney Greenblat and Deena Lebow in New York's Soho. THE CENTER OF THEIR HOME IS THIS SPECTACULAR WOODEN TABLE, WHICH HAS A GLASS TOP COVERING VARIOUS SCULPTED OBJECTS. IT WAS DESIGNED BY THE WELL-KNOWN SCULPTOR AND PRINTMAKER GIUSEPPE ROMEO. In the 1990s, he made a series of distressed modified sculptural furniture, and created this table especially for Rodney

and Deena. They love it, using it all the time for family meals and entertaining friends. ITS UNIQUENESS MAKES IT A REAL CONVERSATION PIECE BUT, IN SPITE OF THIS, IT FITS IN REALLY WELL AMONG THE COUPLE'S COLLECTION OF ART. Rodney is world-famous for his whimsical artwork, and the apartment is full of the most extraordinary paintings, furniture, and decorations. It is a truly eclectic space, reflecting the owners' artistic vision.

▲ This expressive room shows how Rodney and Deena actually live among their fanciful art. Center stage is the sculpted table but it faces stiff competition from the surrounding bright colors.

⬆ Seen from above, this festive
table looks spectacular. The
display revolves around long,
slender branches from the garden.
Glass baubles nestle among them,
while Russian nesting dolls hang
from them. Candlelight imparts
a subtle glow to the setting.

⮞⮞ In my view, you can never have
too many candles. Tiny tea lights
and candles in all shapes, sizes,
and colors light up this festive
table, and bring a touch of magic.

Glassware gives added elegance to this softly lit dining room of muted tones, with the twinkling candlesticks and chandelier helping to create a strong and dramatic atmosphere. Reflecting it all is the handsome antique mirror at one end of the room.

➤➤ Seen through flickering candlelight, the linen napkins rolled in leaf-shaped gilt rings, amber wine glasses, gold-trimmed china, and Gothic-style candle holders give this celebration table a bold and mesmerizing appeal.

Atmosphere is all at this special-occasion supper for two, celebrating a birthday, perhaps, or an anniversary. CANDLELIGHT SETS THE TONE, GIVING A MAGICAL AND INTIMATE QUALITY TO THIS TABLE DISPLAY IN A LONDON BAR. Old church pews provide the seating, while a crumpled linen tablecloth, hanging to the floor, offsets their formality to give a soft and casual feel. THE RANDOM PIECES OF GORGEOUS CHINA, COLLECTED OVER TIME BY THE OWNER SIMPLY BECAUSE SHE LIKED THEM, ARE INDIVIDUALLY EXQUISITE BUT TOGETHER THEY ARE BREATHTAKING. The common theme in this collection is gold and, once again, we see how the discipline of collecting in themes makes a decorative story that much stronger.

All the ingredients for a cozy afternoon tea are here. A gold teapot and elegant porcelain cups, together with a crystal cake stand and delicious creamy cakes, are laid out on a tray on top of a linen-covered ottoman. The reclining bronze of a woman is an indicator of how relaxed the occasion will be, while the candlelight and the open fire provide just the right amount of light. And who could overlook Rikki the rescue dog?

This extension to a conservatory has been decorated as a delightful backdrop to the Christmas festivities held in the conservatory proper. The hanging metal basket is an ingenious design, holding a selection of pillar candles in all sizes. When lit, they are reflected in the glass windows and doors, to give a warm, soft glow to the entire space. Additional atmospheric lighting is provided by large pillar candles placed inside the two large glass hurricane lamps on the table. The red glass baubles enveloped in a fir wreath around the lamps appear like glowing embers. Bringing an element of nature to the table are three, large, old Italian olive jars planted with moss and spring bulbs. In the picture below, you can see the Christmas theme continued in the conservatory.

The bold use of the Union flag adds color and fun to this patriotic scene

There's no mistaking the patriotic fervor behind this celebration to mark a royal wedding. The spirit of the occasion has been captured with the bold use of the Union flag in the bunting, tablecloth, and paper napkins. Vintage royal china has been collected in the weeks leading up to the day, but the really special touch is the English trifles in teacups, and cottage pies in mugs.

↑ A table fit to celebrate a royal wedding. Guests are being treated to typically English trifles served in individual vintage teacups. A garnish of blueberries and nuts, topped with a toothpick displaying a London bus, are perfectly judged decorative details.

Keeping it simple and colorful guarantees the success of a little girl's garden party

Pink is the obvious theme for this celebration, from the tablecloth to the cake decoration of roses, picked from the garden, and candles. The color green makes a soothing backdrop.

Color-themed parties are particularly easy to arrange, and WHAT COULD PLEASE A LITTLE GIRL MORE THAN AN ALL-PINK BIRTHDAY PARTY? In the garden of a London bar, the large table has been draped with a neon-pink plastic lace tablecloth. The centerpiece of the celebrations, it displays THE HIGHLIGHT OF THE AFTERNOON: A SIMPLE FROSTED BIRTHDAY CAKE, DECORATED WITH PINK ROSES AND CANDLES. Continuing the theme are pink plants and pink drinks with matching pink straws.

This intimate scene in the conservatory of a London bar has been created for a surprise birthday. Rightly so, the bar is a popular choice for celebrations, as the owner has a keen eye for decoration and the ability to adapt the decor to suit the occasion. THIS IS AN INCREDIBLY ROMANTIC SCENE, WITH ALL THE DETAILS—THE CAKE, THE CANDLES, THE GOLD CHINA—SO PERFECTLY CHOSEN. IT ALL GOES TO PROVE THAT IT'S NOT ALWAYS THE GRAND GESTURES THAT ARE EFFECTIVE, BUT THE CARE TAKEN TO CREATE SOMETHING UNIQUE.

The white-painted raw brick walls have mellowed over time. Reflections add to the mystique of the setting: a huge vintage mirror is reflected in another one opposite, and a large vintage candlestand, which once graced a church, is seen here only as a reflection. The trailing

Surprise your loved one with an understated but delightful birthday tea

▲ Everything about this charming and simple display has been carefully chosen to suit the occasion. Two beautiful rustic candlesticks, gold-colored cups on gold-patterned saucers, and gold cake forks make this celebration very special indeed. Even the homemade cake with cream frosting looks the part.

▨▶ It is the simplicity of the surroundings that has given this conservatory just the right atmosphere for a close and informal birthday celebration. Some inspired and original decoration on the part of the owner has created an unpretentious setting for a relaxed afternoon tea.

ivy, the tall house plant in the corner, and the terracotta wall pot are all reminders that this is a covered garden space, giving a more rustic and relaxed feel.

The atmosphere of this space will gradually change as the daylight fades. The flickering candlelight will be reflected in the mirror and the decorative trailing lights wrapped around the beams and strung below the roof will add to the romance of the occasion. The room is transformed and becomes quite magical.

↑ The room has been set out like an activity center, where the children can sit and create at the make-and-do table, drink and eat, or simply play.

What could be more fun than organizing a party, especially one for small children? The clever way these balloons have been hung, evenly spaced from the ceiling, makes them behave like a kind of canopy over the table below. They are, in effect, upside down, which gives the party a contemporary feel. EVERY ACTIVITY UNDER THE SUN IS HERE TO KEEP THE CHILDREN OCCUPIED, FROM GAMES, TOYS, AND PAINTS TO GLUE, STICKERS, AND FELT. A PAPER TABLECLOTH IS A SENSIBLE PRECAUTIONARY MEASURE BUT DOES NOTHING TO DETRACT FROM THE FUN TO BE HAD ALL AROUND. The setting is suitably bright, cheerful, and jolly. You can really let your imagination run riot with a children's party. Anything goes, and

The calm before the storm: a well-prepared children's party awaiting the guests

don't be scared to use lots of clashing colors to make a more dramatic statement.

Above all, children are easy to please-the colors touch their senses and the addition of plenty of materials for making and creating gets their imaginations working overtime. They will be happily occupied for hours, making for a stress-free party! They won't require any additional stimulation, just plenty of fun food and refreshing juice to fuel them.

↑ ◄ ◼ ▶ ► The activity table has something for every child, from pots of brightly colored Play-Doh and paints to pieces of Lego and multicolored felt shapes. Upside-down balloons make a fun canopy above.

Themed party displays are easy, don't have to be expensive, and provide lots of room for creative minds. This table set for Halloween is ghoulish and scary. Small hands have been covered in red paint and pressed onto paper plates for a gruesome effect, while monster masks, inky black drinks, windfall apples, and fall leaves provide the rest of the props to create the right party atmosphere.

everyone loves ginger beer

➤➤ **A spotted cloth is perfect** for this party table, laden with brightly colored cups, drinks, cookies, and strawberries—all chosen for color and fun. Let the children do their own thing, while you sit back and watch.

Clever creative detail is shown in this display setting for a children's party. THE PLANNING AND CARE THAT HAS BEEN TAKEN IS VERY EVIDENT, AND LOTS OF GOOD IDEAS CAN SPRING FROM THESE PICTURES. THE SCENE, SADLY, IS NOT TO LAST BUT IT IS ONE THAT WILL GIVE A HUGE AMOUNT OF FUN TO EVERYONE INVOLVED. All the elements required for a successful party, including plenty of children's favorites, such as frosted cookies, pink lemonade, and potato chips, are here. If children are older, serve drinks in glass jars with straws for an informal, individual flavor. LET FAVORITE CHARACTERS AND TOYS JOIN THE PARTY, TOO—THE MORE, THE MERRIER!

⬆⬆ Cut out colorful paper word clouds and write fun messages on them. Bring out your child's favorite toys, such as a money box and an ugly doll. Use a spotty teapot for juice, and jazzy colored straws. When planning this kind of event, my motto definitely is "more is more!"

➤➤ Create a visually stimulating environment that helps children use their imaginations, and encourage art and crafts by providing lots of materials for making letters, drawings, and cards. No one could possibly get bored.

←◄ An antique Chinese rice carrier makes a fitting container for the various utensils, oils, and condiments used in this ultra-modern, steel and concrete kitchen. Made of wood and gently curving, the tub is a contrasting element, as are the rusty letters running along the back of the worktop. Spelling Santa's catchphrase "Ho Ho Ho", they are a very cool Christmas decoration, and let us know that the owner has a sense of humor and a love of the unexpected.

▣► Holiday decorations sit side by side with chic interior design. A large, white-glazed olive jar holds a real tree, simply adorned with white frosted baubles. Below, white tea lights give a delicate glow in the late afternoon light.

CHAPTER 6

Whether you're lucky enough to be living high in the hills, surrounded by breathtaking views, or your outdoor space is much more modest, such as a tiny balcony of potted plants, USE NATURE AT EVERY OPPORTUNITY IN YOUR DISPLAYS—IT'S GOOD FOR THE SOUL.

▲ Each place setting is like a rustic still-life, with a dark wicker placemat holding a ridged glass plate, a single violet in a tiny terracotta pot, and a white linen napkin tied with a length of ivy.

◄ As orange as the setting sun, the cotton damask tablecloth makes a vibrant backdrop to the terracotta pots, woodne bowls, and the pitcher on this outdoor dining table. The earthy colors of the cushions on the green garden seat continue the nature-inspired theme.

► Central to the decorative scheme of this small London garden is a white metal table, almost invisible under the glorious display of potted plants. The best of the season, the display shows a flair for color and planting.

Nature's decoration becomes the soothing backdrop for both of these settings

Like a sweeping curtain, the branches of the tree on the left become the canopy above well-used table and chairs, providing welcome respite from the sun. A CARAFE OF WINE AND A BOWL OF NUTS ARE THE ONLY EXTRAS NEEDED TO ENJOY THE SIMPLE PLEASURES OF THIS SETTING IN THE SOUTH OF FRANCE.

THE BACKDROP TO THE SMALL LA TERRACE OPPOSITE IS ALTOGETHER MORE EXOTIC, ENHANCED BY THE MOROCCAN HANGING LAMPS AND CERAMIC-INLAID TABLE. Nevertheless, the atmosphere created by the jungle-like vegetation is also one of calm and relaxation.

➤➤ A table rusted with time looks so right nestled in a secluded part of this garden. The low hanging branches of the tree provide a natural canopy of shade.

➤➤ ➤➤ Three different styles of Moroccan lamps hang from the roof of this terrace, and are perfectly matched with the decorative table and chairs. Exotic plants provided an atmospheric backdrop.

A terrace on the top floor of this converted barn in France is attached to the master bedroom, and provides the perfect spot for afternoon tea. THE VIEW IS SECOND TO NONE, WHICH IS WHY, OF COURSE, THE OWNERS HAVE CHOSEN TO LIVE HERE, HIGH IN THE HILLS. THESE INFORMAL, INTIMATE OCCASIONS ARE VERY PRECIOUS AND A CONSTANT REMINDER OF THE NATURAL BEAUTY SURROUNDING THEM.

The sky-blue-painted shutters, now peeling with age from the combined effects of sun, rain, and snow, contrast with the big blowsy roses picked fresh from the garden. The metal garden table and chairs are painted white, creating another striking block of color, which contrasts with the lush shades of green spread out in the hills and forest beyond. With no other dwelling for miles around, the sense of seclusion is complete.

◄ This table display appears simplicity itself but the devil is in the detail. Vintage cups and saucers collected from local brocantes, homemade cupcakes on a plain, white cakestand, lace napkins, and bone-handled forks, as well as delicately scented garden roses, create a harmonious and relaxing setting.

➤ Peering through the linen curtains of the bedroom, there is nothing to see in the distance other than the hills, forest, and sky—the perfect view to contemplate over afternoon tea.

↑ **A** white metal chair, a napkin cut from an
◄ old rice sack and lined with a white paper
napkin, a pear on a small terracotta dish, a
wicker-encased glass tumbler—all these
elements combine perfectly at this quiet
outdoor table setting.

↑ ➤► **A** delightful place card created from a
◄ pear tied with a luggage label around its stalk.

◄◄ The weathered table and bench form the
foundations for this simple lunch, while the white,
curlicue chairs provide the decoration and bring
light into an otherwise quite gloomy space.

An old stone wall provides shelter and a solid
backdrop for this plain lunch, in keeping with
the unpainted wood of the seasoned table and
bench. ALTHOUGH THE ELEMENTS THAT MAKE UP
THE TABLE DISPLAY, FROM TERRACOTTA AND HEMP
TO WICKER AND STRING, MAY BE CONSIDERED ROUGH
AND UNSOPHISTICATED, THEY ARE TOTALLY CHARMING
IN THIS ENVIRONMENT. IN SPITE OF THE MODESTY OF THE
SCENE, THERE IS NO DOUBT THAT GREAT CARE HAS GONE INTO ITS
CREATION. And who could help but feel special when
greeted by a handwritten place card tied with
string around a pear?

▲▲ ☞→ A moss-covered stone bench acts as the table for
▲▲ a relaxing lunch of wine and cheese in this natural setting.
Two plump, striped floor cushions in natural tones ensure
complete comfort.

Although these photographs depict
a lush pastoral scene at the start of
summer, where NATURE EXTENDS AS FAR
AS THE EYE CAN SEE, WHAT HAS BEEN
CREATED IS SOMETHING INCREDIBLY
INTIMATE. Beside the pond in this
large ramshackle garden is the setting
for an unfussy lunch of cheese and
wine–it is ALMOST AS IF YOU ARE JOINING
NATURE FOR A DRINK.

An private scene of relaxation in a ramshackle French garden

SURPRISE OUTDOOR CELEBRATIONS EARLY IN THE YEAR, WHEN THE WEATHER IS UNEXPECTEDLY WARM, ARE AN ABSOLUTE DELIGHT AND A TASTE OF THINGS TO COME. Here, in this romantic corner of a garden, high in the hills in southwest France and surrounded by trees, a table has been set for an impromptu birthday lunch.

BRIGHT COLORS FOR THE DECORATIONS SET THE TONE. ALONGSIDE PATTERNED PAPER LANTERNS IN COMPLEMENTARY COLORS, A GARLAND OF PAPER BUTTERFLIES IN CLASHING PINK AND TURQUOISE HERALDS THE OCCASION. When the wind blows, they rustle gently and give the soothing effect of movement. The table setting is equally vibrant, displayed

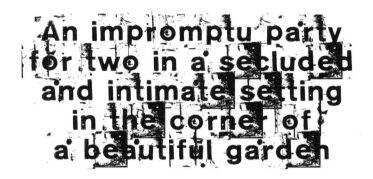

An impromptu party for two in a secluded and intimate setting in the corner of a beautiful garden

A white, metal garden table, with matching curlicue chairs, is perfect to dress up in bright colors for an impromptu party for two. Alongside paper lanterns, a paper butterfly garland, hanging between the branches, flutters in the breeze, creating a mesmerizing haze of color. Cocktail umbrellas and neon-colored straws round off the celebratory atmosphere perfectly.

with bright yellow china, spotted cups, and a large blue enamel pitcher filled with pink and crimson flowers picked from the garden. Party cocktails in tall glasses, neon cardboard name tags, and colored toothpicks are the festive finishing touches.

SPEND TIME LOOKING AROUND YOUR GARDEN IN ORDER TO FIND THE PERFECT SPOT. Here, the low-hanging branches, almost bowing down to the ground, create a MAGICAL, MYSTICAL, ENCLOSED PLACE. The sun shining through the leaves and the surrounding trees all add to the atmosphere.

▼ ➤➤ ➤➤ ➤➤ Perched on the top of a hill, an old marron shed has the perfect view of the surrounding countryside. A table has been fashioned from a well-worn door and the inside of a roll of Tarmac. The original features of the door—the hinges, the grain of the wood, and the marks made during its past life—give character to the table and are the reasons why it works so well in this country setting.

In such a beautiful setting, even the task of chopping wood can't be too arduous. ON THE PORCH OF AN OLD MARRON SHED, ORIGINALLY USED TO STORE CHESTNUTS BUT NOW A WOOD STORE, A TABLE HAS BEEN PUT TOGETHER FROM AN OLD DOOR BALANCED ON A CROSS OF WOOD, ONCE THE INSIDE OF A ROLL OF TARMAC. Simplicity itself, the table seems as if it has always belonged here. To sit down here for a lunch of saucisson and beer, while gazing at the wooded landscape beyond, is sheer bliss. Chopping wood, sipping beer, taking in the view-pause and enjoy!

◄━ The Victorian wall of a London garden is the backdrop to this informal setting. A vintage metal lounger with two cushions provides a spot for relaxation while sipping lemonade. The table is made from a sheet of glass sitting on top of four old stone columns— a clever idea, yet it couldn't be simpler.

➤➤ On a weathered deck in a Brooklyn garden, an intriguing twig-and-branch garden plinth acts as an altar to this plant.

◄◄◄ In the tiny garden of her Hollywood home, the owner has created this prsonal space for reflection, using nature and objects that have special meaning for her and inspire a sense of calm. The bronze statue of Krishna playing the flute conveys a sense of her spirituality.

Making the most of her minuscule garden, the owner of the space opposite has used an old wooden bench with green peeling paint to make a kind of shrine-**A PLACE FOR QUIET REFLECTION AWAY FROM THE NOISE AND BUZZ OF HOLLYWOOD**, where she lives. To help create the right atmosphere, she has embraced nature with potted and climbing plants. THE RUSTY METAL LANTERN ILLUMINATES DARK EVENINGS, INCREASING THE SENSE OF SPIRITUALITY.

A striking garden table made from the intricate branches of a tree

↑ A sackcloth-covered cushion is all that's needed to make this old bench with peeling paint a comfortable place to take a break from gardening.

➤➤ Escaping the Californian sun, Luna, the German Shepherd dog, relaxes on a carved Indian bench under the trees.

These two gardens are quite different in style but both provide a relaxing corner for their owners. On the right, Luna seems to have taken over one of the carved Indian benches for herself. ALTHOUGH IT APPEARS QUITE RURAL, THE GARDEN ABOVE IS IN LONDON. A beaten old bench provides a restful place to enjoy a lunch of bread and jam and an apple.

Two French gardens, one in the heart of the city, the other deep in the country, reflect their owners' simple tastes

In the picture on the left, a bench placed on the side of the hill makes the perfect spot to take in the view or rest from the toil of gardening. FITTING IN SO NATURALLY WITH THE SURROUNDING LANDSCAPE IS THE TABLE ALONGSIDE, MADE OF NOTHING MORE THAN AN OLD DOOR RESTING ON TOP OF A CRATE. The enclosed Parisian garden, above, makes a stunning setting for an informal lunch eaten at a vintage wooden table. All the windows from the house look out onto this calm city garden-the perfect place to shake off the stress of the Paris streets.

A discarded door, balanced on top of a crate, becomes a side table, although the village cat has other ideas!

A watering can filled with a display of wildly trailing plants adds to the charm of the table set for a light summer meal.

A white, slatted wooden table has been made ready for summer drinks, although the weather seems to have other ideas. The extremely useful straw umbrella provides shelter, come rain or shine.

This remote location makes a dramatic setting for evening drinks. Two distant lights are the only signs of other inhabitants.

These are the most dramatic skies, photographed at different times of the day. To the left, THE DARKENING SKY IS THREATENING A STORM, MAKING A STRONG CONTRAST WITH THE STRAW UMBRELLA THAT BRIGHTENS UP THIS CASUAL SETTING. THE FADING LIGHT IN THE PICTURE ON THE RIGHT GIVES THE SCENE AN OVERWHELMING BEAUTY. A table has been set for a late evening drink in the middle of the garden, illuminated by two candelabras burning bright.

A well-designed garden that flows from one set to another, from the formal rose garden through the arch to a secluded dining area

In this lush green setting of an English country garden, trees overhang the round metal table set for lunch, providing welcome shade. TABLE DECORATION IS KEPT TO A MINIMUM, WITH A POT OF HERBS AS THE CENTERPIECE. SCULPTED, RIBBON-LIKE METAL CHAIRS WITH CUSHIONS PROVIDE COMFORTABLE SEATING. LEADING TO THE TABLE IS A WINDING PATH FRAMED WITH IMPRESSIVELY MANICURED BOX PLANTS IN STATELY TERRACOTTA POTS. Strategically placed among them are metal, globe-shaped candle holders, ready to provide light once the sun goes down.

▲ ←◀ An archway of roses acts as
a kind of doorway to the dining
area of the garden. The round table
on the raised stone patio is set for
lunch, with the box plants and candle
holders giving a contemporary feel.

▲ This impromptu table has been
fashioned out of the bottom half
of a metal barrel barbecue, with a
chopping board added to provide
a stable surface. Ivy and Fio,
meanwhile, anticipate a treat.

▶▶ A zinc table, with a stone bust
surrounded by potted herbs, makes
a carefully thought-out and striking
garden display. The metal candle
holder hanging from the canopy roof
is not only practical but also adds
balance to this well-designed space.

WATER PROVIDES THE SETTING AND SPECTACULAR BACKDROP FOR THIS BEACH SETTING. The aim of the outdoor breakfast table in Malibu is to RELAX IN STYLE AND ENJOY BEING BY THE SEA. As this picture shows, this has been achieved beyond any reasonable doubt and by the simplest means. What better place to enjoy a leisurely weekend breakfast, or to WATCH THE SUN GO DOWN OVER THE HORIZON? Blue and white always make perfect partners, and here an undemanding table setting of well laundered and softly crumpled chair covers and tablecloth and mismatched vintage tableware enhances rather than detracts from the expanse of clear blue sea seen beyond the vast picture windows.

➤ A white tablecloth and slipcovers introduce a touch of elegance to this relaxing outdoor breakfast at Rachel Ashwell's beachside house in Malibu. The warm Californian sun filters through the lattice roof, while the ocean provides breathtaking scenery.

INDEX

PICTURE CREDITS

Marie-France Cohen
(www.merci-merci.com)
2/3, 6/7, 8, 12/13, 15,
56/57, 58/59, 60/61,
62/63, 64/65, 66/67,
70/71, 74 middle,
104/105, 106/107,
111 bottom, 161, 215

Paul and Tina Curtin
4, 27, 36, 46 left,
84/85, 94/95, 152/153,
196, 198/199, 200/201,
202/203, 204/205,
216/217

Anne and Peter Rivett
9, 72, 73, 100/101,
172/173

**Mick Lindberg and
Arun Soni**
10, 110/111, 142/143,
162

**Lisa Arden and
David George**
14, 19, 66/67, 146, 197

Lisa Carrier
16/17, 18, 20/21,
118/119, 212/213

Michael Reeves
(www.michaelreevesassociates.
co.uk)
16, 26, 45 right, 48
left, 49 right, 77
middle, 82/83, 151

Christine Innamorato
11, 140

**Trevor Halls and
Mark Cooke**
22, 43 top, 46 middle,
76, 86, 147, 195

Marilyn and Julyan Day
22, 24/25, 28, 31/32,
44, 46 left, 88/89,
96/97, 168/169,
176/177, 178, 179,
192/193, 218/219

Rachel Ashwell
(www.rachelashwellshabbychic
couture.com)
29, 33, 35, 40 middle
left, 43 bottom, 45
middle, 47 right,
50 left, 77 right,
90/91, 92/93, 112/113,
114/115, 166/167, 221

Donna Walker
(www.donnawalker.org)
78/79

Lily Ashwell
(www.lilyashwell.com)
116/117

Abigail Aked
(www.abigailaked.co.uk)
124/125

Liddie and Howard Harrison
(www.holtharrison.co.uk)
130, 149, 150

Oana Camilleri
(www.oanacamilleri.blogspot.com)
132

Emma Gibson
(www.egibson.co.uk)
128/129, 134 middle

Portia Barnett-Herrin
115

Alex Starck
134 left and far right

Nicky Butler
34, 37, 41, 51, 52, 81

Ron and Stacy Robinson
39, 42, 48 middle, 87
right

Fran Macmillan
(www.metroclapham.com)
53, 80, 174/175, 182,
184/185

**Laurence Amélie and
Ubaldo Franceschini**
(www.laurence-amelie.com)
(www.ubaldo-franceschini.
blogspot.com)
74, 108/109, 120/121,
122/123, 141 right,
170/171

Beverley Pond-Jones
86, 126/127, 156/157

The Detiger family
(www.jonnydetiger.com)
102, 103, 160 left

Michele Matthewman
103 bottom

Geraldine James
44, 145, 146, 155,
180/181, 194, 208/209,
212

Casper Slieker
(www.casperslieker.com)
38, 54/55, 98/99

Adam Towner
(www.thedeaddollsclub.com)
144, 148, 158/159, 163

**Rodney Greenblat and
Deena Lebow**
(www.whimsyload.com)
164/165

Lee Curtis
186/187, 188/189, 190,
191

Ian Wallace
136/137, 138/139

Patrick and Christina Shaw
211

ACKNOWLEDGMENTS

I would like to thank Cindy Richards, Gillian Haslam, and Sally Powell from CICO Books, for all their support and guidance throughout the making of this book. To Paul Tilby for his awesome creative skill with the layout, and Helen Ridge for all her help with the text.

A great big, special thanks to Andrew Wood, of course, for the wonderful photographs and the massive support during our second adventure together, and for sharing this creative journey into people's lives and homes with me, and meeting all these incredibly generous people.

To Rachel Ashwell, for generously inviting us to her beautiful homes in California; Laurence Amélie and Ubaldo Franceschini, for not only giving us shelter but also introducing us to the amazing Marie-France Cohen, who graciously allowed us into her two enchanting homes.

To Paul and Tina Curtin, for all the endless possibilities in their magical mountaintop home; Marilyn and Julyan Day, for winter and summer pictures in the UK and summer ones in France-that's just greedy!

To Rick and Debra Haylor, for their continued support; Lee Curtis, for once again bringing it out of the bag; Emma Gibson, for taking me into her crazy world; Nicky Butler, for generously introducing us to his cool friends.

To Robert Falconer and Louise Ames, who never moan when I am being a pain.

Thank you to Rosie, my daughter, who is a big fan and a big support.

Rosie and I would like to dedicate this book to Rikki, our dog, who died earlier this year at 19 years old. She was a great friend and we miss her massively. She even made it into this book, on pages 176-7. Her mates at the dogs' home would be impressed!